56930

A Practical Guide to the Conduct of Field Research in the Social Sciences

Other Titles of Interest

The Modern Middle East: A Guide to Research Tools in the Social Sciences, Reeva S. Simon

International Terrorism: An Annotated Bibliography and Research Guide, Augustus R. Norton and Martin H. Greenberg

Bibliography on World Conflict and Peace: Second Edition, Elise Boulding, J. Robert Passmore, and Robert Scott Gassler

Aging and the Aged: An Annotated Bibliography and Library Research Guide, Linna Funk Place, Linda Parker, and Forrest J. Berghorn

African International Relations: An Annotated Bibliography, Mark W. DeLancey

A Select Bibliography on Economic Development: With Annotations, John P. Powelson

National Planning in the United States: An Annotated Bibliography, David E. Wilson

About the Book and Author

A Practical Guide to the Conduct of Field Research in the Social Sciences

Elliot J. Feldman

This book offers students in the social sciences simply stated, direct guidance in defining problems for research and in organizing and conducting a research program. Confronting philosophical and practical problems, it will serve both graduate and undergraduate students well, providing the former with assistance in preparing their theses and informing the latter on how to develop research papers. Dr. Feldman addresses basic questions about topic selection, interviewing, surveys, documentation, and other research methods. While his emphasis is on comparative research, any student pursuing field research in political science, sociology, anthropology, geography, social psychology, and other branches of the social sciences will find the book helpful. The concentration on data collection, rather than analysis, will make it particularly useful for those undertaking a research project for the first time.

Elliot J. Feldman, director of the University Consortium for Research on North America, is assistant professor of politics at Brandeis University and research associate at the Harvard University Center for International Affairs. Dr. Feldman was formerly visiting assistant professor of policy analysis at the University of British Columbia and was assistant professor of European politics and political science at the Johns Hopkins University School of Advanced International Studies. A former Woodrow Wilson Fellow, Dr. Feldman has also received fellowships from The Fund for Peace, the German Marshall Fund of the United States, and the United States Arms Control and Disarmament Agency.

A Practical Guide to the Conduct of Field Research in the Social Sciences

Elliot J. Feldman

Westview Press / Boulder, Colorado

Copyright © 1981 by Westview Press, Inc.

Published in 1981 in the United States of America by
Westview Press, Inc.
5500 Central Avenue
Boulder, Colorado 80301
Frederick A. Praeger, Publisher

Library of Congress Cataloging in Publication Data
Feldman, Elliot J.
A practical guide to the conduct of field research in the social sciences.
Bibliography: p.
1. Social sciences—Field work. I. Title.
H61.F37   300'.723   80-15796
ISBN 0-89158-980-5
ISBN 0-89158-981-3 (pbk.)

Printed and bound in the United States of America

For Gilbert F. White and Theodore J. Lowi,
scholars who have been my teachers and friends

Contents

Foreword

Many research workers in social science will be skeptical about the need for a guide to the conduct of field studies. Some may argue that the apprentice investigator can learn best at the elbow of the seasoned scientist or by trial and error. And it will be asserted that an abundant number of disciplinary treatises and handbooks on study methods are already available.

A few years ago I would have been inclined to place less emphasis upon the utility of writing down rudimentary suggestions. There is a kind of mystical belief among certain field workers that they have learned the art and can communicate it to others through association on the job. They consider that little else is required.

As I look over the results of a goodly number of recent studies I conclude that this skepticism is unwarranted in most instances. The record shows that some field investigations have gone astray and that Murphy's law has been at work on the very points enumerated by Elliot Feldman. More than a few young social scientists are going into unfamiliar field situations without adequate preparation. Much of the literature on methodology in anthropology, geography, political science, psychology, and sociology appraises the issues involved in approaches to interviewing and observation. However, these treatises more often deal with such questions as the validity of interview responses and the danger of impressing an external view on a local culture than with the more earthy problems of planning and carrying out the study. In addition to dealing with these problems, Feldman looks at the extremely sensitive and complex ethical issues of inquiring into individual and community lives.

I strongly recommend that any young investigator contemplating going into the field take a look at the Feldman guide. The book also makes a convenient checklist for the old hand, and it is likely to suggest points that may otherwise be overlooked. Even if it illuminates no new techniques for the experienced researcher, it will underline the basic importance of high-quality data and the way in which field technique determines the validity of the data. All too often broad generalizations and sophisticated analysis are based on data drawn from casual and inaccurate information obtained through inquiry on the ground.

The guide draws heavily upon two lines of investigation that have been expanding and in which Feldman and his colleagues have been most active. One is the growing emphasis upon policy-oriented research, which typically is interdisciplinary. The other is the interest in comparative studies across cultural and political boundaries. Such studies tend to involve collaboration with local residents. Both types of research may call upon field workers with different experience and training. For them, a few common ground rules may be helpful, and a simplified and direct review of lessons may be especially important in assuring valid and precise information.

The questions raised by Feldman inevitably arise in the course of field study. Better they do so sooner than too late.

Gilbert F. White
Institute of Behavioral Science
University of Colorado at Boulder

Preface

Social science research has long been regarded as mysterious. There always has been an apparent need or desire to give to social science research the scientific legitimacy normally attributed to laboratory work. To this end, social scientists frequently have been vague about exactly what they do and exactly how they get their information. When not vague, explanations are so frequently laden with jargon that even other social scientists cannot figure out what is being done.

The objective of this book is to demystify one area of social science research—field research—by describing in simple terms what it is and some of the ways in which it can be pursued effectively. Three areas of social science field research have received substantial treatment in the past: the work of anthropologists, the work of sociologists, and the work of behavioral scientists refining surveys. My own orientation is toward policy research, and I have given this volume a modest bias accordingly. Furthermore, since the value of comparative research is becoming more fully recognized, I have decided to discuss field research problems often in terms of comparative efforts. The difficulties and advantages of comparative research are poorly understood, the special features of comparative research nowhere articulated. Despite these two biases, however, the discussion here ought to serve all social science field research.[1]

This volume is a "handbook," a volume of "how to." Social science graduate students frequently complain of two principal deficiencies in their education: (1) they receive role models but little or no guidance in how to teach; and (2) they receive countless examples of research but little or no guidance in how to conduct research themselves. They are asked to find out things, but they are rarely told where to look or how to find out. When they set out on master's and doctoral theses, they all too frequently find themselves in the field uncertain of what to do. Many social scientists have suggested to me that up to three months of settling down and getting acquainted should always be allowed before serious research can begin. In the days when grant money was more abundant and few felt rushed to complete their degrees, such an assertion was especially convenient for foreign vacations. My own experience in the field tells me that the disorientation is more the consequence of ignorance than of natural causes, that it is not always a necessary feature of research, and that, to a large extent, it can be avoided.

It is certainly true that every research project is different, that every individual who conducts research will have peculiar personal qualities that affect procedures, and that every locus of research dictates particular needs. It is also true that some places take more getting used to and that some kinds of projects require a slower pace than others. My own research has taken me to five foreign countries and six different regions of the United States. I have found that, despite the peculiarities, certain general factors emerge that can be applied to almost all settings and situations. From this experience, and from discussion with colleagues also engaged in field research, I have concluded that this "practical guide," at least for the advanced industrial world, has a universal application.

Some of the suggestions will raise complex and serious moral questions. Because this book is intended as a practical guide and not as a philosophical treatise, I will point out where I think moral issues are involved but will not discuss these issues. They are surely appropriate subjects for concerned discussion and debate, and they are not ignored here as if to suggest that they should be avoided. Rather, it is up to each researcher to evaluate moral implications in a given case. A practical guide, unfortunately, can do no more than point out where what is practical may not necessarily be ethical. I think I would be remiss if, because in some instances ethical judgment would discard apparently practical solutions to problems, I therefore failed to suggest, for all cases, practical solutions. This choice, too, of course, may be criticized, but it is a choice I make in an effort to be honest and consistent in the fulfillment of the objectives of this guide.

This book emphasizes data collection, not analysis. The behavioral literature is concerned more with analysis, but as we shall see, serious doubts are raised over the quality of data. Hence, behavioralists, whose basic inclinations may differ from my own, may at least pause here to reconsider the source of the numbers on which they so heavily rely.

In the field, numerous problems arise that seem peculiar. This guide should reduce the number of apparently peculiar problems by indicating that many such problems arise elsewhere, have been experienced by others, and tend toward a general solution. Not all suggestions here should necessarily be followed. The researcher's own intuition may in the end be the best guide. Nevertheless, the weight of experience has proven the worth of many solutions proposed here.

Although this volume makes particular reference to field research, I want to emphasize that it should be useful to all social scientists who leave their libraries (and more recently their laboratories) to collect data. The examples used are all drawn from my personal research experience and occasionally the experience of colleagues, which means they are real, not abstract, examples. Furthermore, I have attempted to put things in simple—even inelegant—terms, for I do not attempt here to justify or to defend field research, but rather to provide some guidance for it. The novice then may accelerate in becoming expert by using this guide. Those uncomfortable, and often unprofitable, first months of quiet desperation may be better managed in light of another's experience. And I hope the experience of new research will bring from some reader a new guide with better tips and more helpful information. The ultimate objective is to expand the number and improve the quality of people conducting field research in social science, so that we may know more, sooner, about our social, political, and economic world.

Elliot J. Feldman

Notes

1. Eugene Bardach has argued that the requirements of policy research differ from those of other social sciences. In some respects (due especially to short deadlines and political volatility) policy research does impose different requirements, as in lining up expert defenders and timing carefully the release of results. Nevertheless, the similarities far outweigh the differences, and experiences are applicable across the social science disciplines. See Eugene Bardach, "Gathering Data for Policy Research," *Urban Analysis* 2 (1974): 117–144.

Acknowledgments

I have been fortunate to have had the opportunity to test the effectiveness of these ideas on students of four different levels in three different institutions of higher education. Originally developed as a series of lectures in 1974, the manuscript underwent changes based on what students found difficult to understand and put into practice. At the Johns Hopkins School of Advanced International Studies, master's candidates used the presentation as an introduction before conducting intensive field research on airport development and citizen participation in Milan and Paris; at the University of British Columbia, fifth-year commerce students followed these guidelines for a series of team field projects in Vancouver; at Brandeis University, a team of undergraduates, ranging from sophomores to seniors, put the suggestions here into practice on the common problem of solid waste disposal in Greater Boston, and their efforts were followed by a similar team of doctoral candidates. In each instance I was able to profit from their experience and further refine and improve the presentation.

Liz Shultis and Alice Levine of Westview Press have contributed unerring professional advice for achieving order and clarity without ever losing the spirit or style of a teaching book. A number of scholars, in addition, have provided thoughtful and useful ideas for the manuscript. Gilbert F. White of the University of Colorado first taught me the joy of field research and was the first to give the manuscript a sympathetic and useful reading. Others who contributed significantly to a final version include Theodore J. Lowi of Cornell University, Jerome Milch of the University of Pittsburgh, Stephen Weinberger of Dickinson College, Bill Zumeta of UCLA, Peter Sheras of the

University of Virginia, and Clark Gilmour of the University of British Columbia. This list includes scholars in political science, geography, history, psychology, business, and policy analysis. But the most valuable observations came inevitably from my wife, Lily Gardner Feldman, whose own sensitivity to students and their needs helped me to seek out the clearest phrases and the most intelligible examples. Whatever remains unclear or incorrect is my own fault.

E.J.F.

A Practical Guide to the Conduct of Field Research in the Social Sciences

1
Choosing Subjects and Objects of Research

What is research? What does it mean to do research? Let us agree that a directed inquiry involving evidence that must be gathered—not just intuited—is research. Research involves the collection of information for some specific purpose associated with answering questions, solving problems, or generating understandings. We undertake research in order to know, to understand, to explain, or to predict—or all of these things or some of them. The key, however, is that research is a purposeful task.

The wonders and the ills of the world present us with more than enough questions to occupy us superficially for many lifetimes. If we choose to inquire—that is, if we are inclined to research—how do we decide what to do research on? For our purposes, there are three pertinent responses to this question. The first is that we are engaged in research within the disciplines of social science. We each have our own peculiar explanations for why we engage in social science research instead of, say, the study of the atom. I will not try to answer here why we do this kind of research; let it suffice that we have made this particular disciplinary choice our first premise. But, given that premise, what do we mean by it? That is, what is social science research?

Let us agree that by social science research we mean the inquiry into problems involving human and institutional interaction. More particularly, I am referring to research concerned with the way men and women interact, as individuals and as groups, and with the way they structure their governments for the purpose of managing, guiding, and directing their public affairs. Social scientists are concerned with individual, group, and institutional goals and processes and with what men and women seek and how their aims are pursued individually and through institutions. Research into social activity—whether political or economic—is social science research.

Given that we are engaged in social science research, two responses remain to the question "How do we decide what to do research on?" One response concerns the questions we ask, the *subject* for our inquiry: What do we want to know about? The other response concerns the vehicle for the subject, which is the *object* of research: How will we find out about it?

Choosing a Topic

The choice of a research topic is intensely personal. Choices are made consciously, half-consciously, subconsciously, and unconsciously, and the quality of the research, in the long run, may well correspond to the kinds of choices we have made. You can best choose a topic by asking: What is most important to me? What question would I most like answered? Obviously, there are some boundaries within which such questions must be posed. If you declare that what interests you most is the meaning of life, you will be hard-pressed to pursue an effective program of research. However, there is an order of inquiry that will guide you to discover just how narrow your question must be. Once you have asked your question—that is, once you have defined your subject—you must then ask, "What will I do to find the answer?"

Effective research is systematic. Traveling as far as possible for as long as possible may be a popular method for investigating the meaning of life, but it will not qualify as a program of research. What questions, exactly, will we ask? Where? Of whom? On our travels, to whom will we speak? Our mortality obliges us to appreciate that our time is limited. We cannot speak to everyone. We must choose among the multitudes. What will be the basis of our choices? Shall we speak only to the rich? Only to the poor? Only to the powerful? Only to the weak? To some of each? Shall we sample opinion? How many views in each category shall we solicit? As soon as we begin asking these kinds of questions, we cannot help but discover that (1) we must be selective, and (2) we must be systematic. These two discoveries must guide the rest of our inquiry.

The subject of research should be something of personal importance or consequence. It is true that what is important to us may not be important to others, but because it is important to us, we can hope to be committed and to persevere when the answers seem few and the questions seem to multiply. Pursuing personal interests does, however, carry with it a problem involving the values we bring to bear in the very choices we make. We must consider carefully why something seems important to us and whether its importance is generated by selfish interests, by intellectual curiosity—or by both. There is no harm in pursuing research generated out of selfish interest, but there *is* harm in not being aware of our own motivations. We must separate our selfish interests from the systematic task and make every effort to suspend our judgments while selecting evidence. We might set out to prove something, but only the evidence—and not our own interests—can ultimately prove it. If we delude ourselves into accepting certain conclusions before the evidence is gathered, the research is destined to fail.

The distinction here is a very important one. Our research is committed because we choose both subject and object, but we cannot predetermine or prejudge the outcome of our inquiry. Our research is ideological because we choose what questions to ask, and our choice of questions cannot help but be a profoundly ideological proposition. Thus, there is no suggestion here that research is value-free. Rather, I am suggesting that in reaching conclusions we must suspend judgment, collecting and weighing evidence with open minds, conscious of the reasons underlying the choices of subject and object that we have already made.

What's First: Subject or Object?

Whether we choose the subject or the object first, the subject must be *matched* with the object. That is, we may not have a burning question we want to answer, such as (a burning question for me, at least) "Why was Weston, Illinois, chosen as the site for an atomic accelerator?" but we might be interested in knowing everything possible about atomic accelerators.[1] The object of our research, then, will be atomic accelerators, and the research will involve collecting all the information we can about these machines. In beginning to assemble this information, we will be obliged to ask a subjective question, for, whereas the object provides the vehicle for data collection, the subjective question is the instrument for putting the information into some kind of order. We will be confronted by what I call the "So what?" of our inquiry. The object may come first, but we must inevitably attach the subject to it if the results are to be reported systematically.

It is not certain, either, whether it is preferable to choose the subject or the object first. But let us consider for a moment what we must do after we have chosen a subject. For research purposes, we probably cannot ask, "What is the meaning of life?" There is nothing wrong with the question, but the method we must adopt to answer it cannot bear up to such breadth or vagueness. Given the constraints on our time, we must select a systematic method for examining the question. That method must involve something or someone. If we ask, "Why was Weston, Illinois, chosen as the site for an atomic accelerator?" we can identify within the question at least four objects for inquiry: the village of Weston, the state of Illinois, atomic accelerators, and choosers of the site. And if we focus our systematic inquiry on these four objects, we are likely to formulate at least some hypothetical answers to our subjective questions. Furthermore, if we ask a broader question, such as "How do sites for science projects get chosen?" it is probable that our case study will lead the way to a tentative answer. For, no matter how broad the question (defining the subject), the answer needs examples. Cases and examples are derived from objects.

Choosing the subject, then, tends to identify the objects for study. We could pose any number of subjective questions in this vein. A question such as "Why do experts exclude ordinary citizens from important technical decisions?" would lead us to examine experts, ordinary citizens, technicians, and technical decisions.[2] "Is conscription necessary to raise an army?" leads us to conscription as a program, necessity as a concept, and armies.[3] In every instance, our first task after posing the subjective question is to ask, "What must we look at in trying to answer this question?"

Choosing the object first is sometimes easier (especially if we do not have any burning conceptual questions of our own), but it is often harder to do effective analysis by proceeding this way. We may sense, for example, that cities are decreasingly habitable, but our vague feelings on the matter may lead simply to a desire to know all about urban planning. If urban planning is to be the object of our inquiry, we must then ask more specifically, "What *about* urban planning?" Ultimately we will have to pose a subjective question. It might be, "Are cities less habitable because of poor urban planning?" or "Could urban planning improve the plight of our cities?" Again, we should seek to identify the object of inquiry by carefully examining the question we pose. If we ask whether cities are less habitable, we will need to examine cities, urban planning, and the concept of habitability. That is, the terms used in asking the question will always determine the first stage of our inquiry. Even if we have started with an object, we must ultimately pose a question about it. The great "So what?" should hang over all research, and it should oblige us to think hard about the "what."

The problem here is not one of merely defining the terms. Rather, it is a problem of grasping concepts. Let us pursue the urban planning example to see how we acquire a focus in our research. What does it mean for a city to be less habitable? For that matter, what kinds of communities shall we include under the name "city?" Shall we choose communities on the basis of geographic size, population size, population density, local law? By determining what it means to be habitable (and, therein, more or less habitable), and by deciding what to include in the category of "city," we are setting down criteria. Those criteria will guide our choice of objects into narrower areas. For example, we may suggest that crime and cleanliness are principal measures of habitability. For the first of these we can seek a variety of statistical measures. We can see whether there are trends in various categories of crime, though we may find ourselves obliged at some point to judge whether the incidence of one crime is preferable (i.e., makes the city more habitable) to the incidence of another. If there are more rapes but fewer armed robberies, for example, is the city becoming more or less habitable? All criteria we choose—and all measures we take—will at some point force us to make judgments of this kind. But we will have other measures—or other criteria—to help us as well. On the matter of cleanliness, we might look at how often a city cleans its streets. We might also ask how good its equipment is and what kind of cleaning it does. Are the streets merely swept, or are they also washed? Is the labor manual or mechanized? Where is garbage dumped, and how often? We will necessarily have to judge whether the city is clean and whether it is getting cleaner or dirtier on the basis of these and other such questions. But we will also be able to use this judgment about cleanliness along with the judgment about crime as we push toward an answer to our original question.

We will seek other measures of habitability, but we will also narrow our scope of object in terms of city. However we choose to define "city," we will need to examine *examples* of cities rather than *all* cities. Furthermore, if we examine more than one city for *relative* habitability, we introduce comparative research. But for just a moment we are getting ahead of ourselves.

I have said that the subject of research must be tied to an object and that if we begin subjectively, the first questions we ask must come directly from our subjective question. In posing the subjective question, we have—whether secretly or openly—created a hypothetical answer. In the question "Could urban planning improve the plight of our cities?" we have already implied that our cities are suffering in some relative way and that urban planning is a possible remedy. Thus, there is an unstated hypothesis that urban planning can or cannot improve cities. Our hypothesis raises innumerable other questions, such as "Who does the planning?" but it is the recognition of the hypothesis that is most important. With that recognition our inquiry becomes all the more purposeful. We seek to prove whether urban planning has a consequence, and, if so, in what way. Our evidence may support or refute the hypothesis, but what is more important is that we are able to formulate the hypothesis in order to guide our inquiry.

The hypothesis—which, if we think about it, inevitably asks whether something is true or is false, is one way or the other—leads implicitly to a model. If urban planning does improve cities, then we can suggest that urban planning is a cause whose effect is better cities. And if we propose the contrary—that urban planning does not improve cities—then we suggest that either (1) cities cannot be improved or (2) forces other than planning will bring improvement. Again, there is an implied causal model. The question ultimately reduces itself to the classic hypothesis: if A then B. If we persist in formulating and reformulating our questions until we recognize the hypotheses and the models implicit in them, we will always find a path along which to pursue our inquiries.

Testing the Hypothesis

Since this book emphasizes comparative research, the comparative method is therefore central to how we will test our hypotheses. Many methods are available, of course,[4] but in every test we need a standard—something against which to measure. Cities are either more or less habitable according to some ad hoc or abstract criteria, or they are more or less habitable relative to each other. In both cases, we judge according to some norm or standard. Comparative research tends to prefer the latter standard—in this case that one city is more or less habitable than another—without precluding the possibility of abstract criteria for judgment. All noncomparative research ultimately depends on abstract or ad hoc criteria. Comparative research seems superior to me because it provides concrete grounds for judgment while improving our awareness of a wider range of choices and possibilities.

No matter what method we choose to use, we must define our terms with some care. To understand what the comparative method is, we must first establish what a method is. In the broadest sense, a method is a way of going about something—usually a problem. It is a way of asking a question, conducting a discussion, observing a phenomenon. A method can also be an instrument or device for testing hypotheses or evaluating information. The identification of a method involves at least two choices. First, the way we go about investigating a problem depends above all on the problem we choose. Second, the method we then choose must in some intelligible way correspond to the problem. This point is not to be taken lightly. Many are the research designs that fail because methods are poorly related to problems.

I would like to emphasize here the notion of choice itself. We must remember that when we choose a problem, we choose one problem among many, and that when we choose a method to solve that problem, we choose one among many possible ways of solving the problem. These choices are value-laden; they carry with them biases and constraints, screening out some possibilities while maximizing others. If, for example, we want to know the impact of a new airport on a community, we may choose to interview community and citizen-group leaders. That is a methodological choice, but we might also choose to examine medical records statistically over time to establish whether health is affected by pollution from the airport. Spokesmen may guess, and doctors may know for their own groups of patients, but only through a thorough examination of all medical records can we verify this information. Even then, not all ill people see doctors, and not all doctors keep good records. Changes in health might be coincidental and not caused by the airport. This information, moreover, only pertains to one aspect of a multifaceted problem. For this aspect we have chosen a method—the inspection of medical records—but there are other aspects that may call for other methods. At some point we must decide—or *choose*—how many aspects are sufficient to determine "impact" and which aspects are the most useful to know. For each of these concerns we must also seek evidence in support of our choices.

Each time we make a choice, then, we involve a method, and each time we involve a method, we make a choice. These methods are instruments—ways of asking and explaining—but they are not value-free. A survey, for example, implies that we trust in some way what people tell us. If we survey prior to an election, we assume people will tell us something useful for predicting how they will behave—that is, how they will vote.

They may in fact vote as we predict, but it is only our *interpretation* of their answers that permits us to claim they voted a certain way for any particular reason. Can we know for sure why people vote as they do? We do not stand in the voting booth and can never know why they make a particular choice when they actually pull the lever. What they tell us may be anything from conjecture to rationalization. When we choose to use a survey, or any other method that relies on unsworn testimony, we must recognize this problem.

Ideally, methods are designed to resolve hypotheses that form predictive models: if A then B. If A is present or occurs, then B also will be present or occur. The ultimate problem lies in the *then*, for even if we are able to predict as the result of experimentation, we cannot explain *why* except through the interpretation of our hypothesis. Had we a paradigm—that is, had we an embracing, testable, and apparently reliable theory with quintessential examples, such as Newton's gravity to explain falling apples—our problem, superficially at least, would be solved. In social science, however, there are competing paradigms; disagreement abounds over valid interpretation and adequate and appropriate evidence. Choices of methods, therefore, are debatable. For all of them there is, at heart, a simple problem: All we have to go on is what is written down, what we ourselves can see and hear, and what people tell us. In the first case we can never know if we have found everything that has been written down. In the second case we can never be sure that our own eyes and ears have provided a full account. And in the third case we can never be absolutely certain that we have been told the truth or that we have compensated for every possible inaccuracy and fallacy. Together these difficulties leave us on uncertain ground. The best research designs, however, seek to minimize these weaknesses by reducing their probability. Minimizing their influence is ultimately the key to good social science.

If a method, then, involves the way a question is asked and the techniques employed to answer it, what does the comparative method involve? If we multiply the difficulties of methods and methodology to however many things we want to compare, we can begin to appreciate the difficulties of the comparative method. In effect, there is no single comparative method. Scholars disagree about appropriate methodology in general, and the comparative method is one of many competitors. In the case of the comparative method, however, there is further disagreement because there are many possible ways to compare. Hence, we have two tasks. We must understand the comparative method as one of many methodologies, and we must establish separately what the—or a—comparative method is itself.

What does it mean to compare? What can be compared? In grammar school we learned not to add apples and oranges except in quantity—yet we were taught to compare them. One was smooth, the other rough; one orange, the other multicolored, and so forth. If we had ten oranges and ten apples, we could generalize only by consolidating categories, reporting that we had twenty pieces of fruit. Ten pears added in would give us thirty pieces of fruit. Now we add ten rocks—that gives us forty what? We compare the ten rocks to the ten apples. We have the same number so we describe their different and relative qualities. In so doing, we choose criteria, and we introduce standards, or norms. We might say, for example, that one is softer than the other; the standard for soft is then the consequence of a norm between the two. Now let us imagine these rather flexible norms in a more political context. If we say that Belgium is more developed than Italy (ignoring the problem of defining "developed"—a problem little different, really, from defining "softness"), we might also note that France is more developed than Belgium, that Germany is more developed than France, and that the United States is more developed than Germany. If the apple is soft, which country is developed?

This problem is inescapable. Social science obliges us to offer definitions and to construct categories. Comparative social science obliges us to distinguish not only among these categories, but also among sets of categories. And so, in the definitions we choose and in the methods we apply, we introduce evidence and interpretation. We make judgments, we display preferences, we make moral commitments. But the comparative method also provides us with standards—at least to the extent that we ensure comparability between and among categories.

We will test our hypotheses, then, by defining criteria that may be applied from one category to another. Given the question "Is airport service in Milan superior to service in other cities in Italy?" we can identify as objects of inquiry airports, airport service, Milan, other Italian cities, the deliverers of services, and criteria for "superiority." We must also recognize that our question is not "Is airport service good in Milan?" This question would require some standard of "good." Our question, in fact, provides a standard, but to answer it we must compare Milan's services to services elsewhere. Thus, we must see to it that (1) by "airport" we mean more or less the same thing in more than one place; and (2) by "service" we refer to phenomena more or less the same from place to place. For these objects, at the very least, we must derive consistent definitions that assume what we measure in Rome is more or less the same as what we measure in Milan. For each item we seek to make comparisons; we also tally within the categories and among the categories from place to place. Given comparable things to measure, we will eventually develop a composite whereby we can seek to answer, finally, the question of whether Milan's airport services are, indeed, superior.[5]

There are really two levels at work here—one related to the subject and the other to the object. Our subjective question, for the purposes of comparative analysis, must have meaning wherever we ask it. This problem is a serious one. When Gabriel Almond and Sidney Verba set out to ask Mexican peasants and German businessmen the same questions, their assumptions about comparability—that the questions would have a common meaning in different cultures, occupations, socioeconomic classes, and languages—necessarily undermined the quality of their study. *The Civic Culture*, although generally regarded as a landmark in comparative research, would serve as well as an example of doubtful methodological assumptions.[6]

Almond and Verba discovered, as we shall discuss later on, that people answer most questions they are asked. However, comparing the answers assumes common questions. Although the questions, to an American scholar, may appear to be the same, once posed through linguistic, cultural, social, economic, and political filters, the questions in one place may bear no resemblance to the questions in another. Even "yes" and "no" can take on different meanings. The question (that is, the subject) must be pertinent in as many places, in as many languages, and in as many cultures and socioeconomic classes as it might be asked. It must be asked by equally skilled interviewers making similar impressions on respondents. If the question is not comparably pertinent, we can only learn which questions are pertinent in different places; our comparison can go no deeper.

Comparability must be assumed at the objective level as well. We might inquire about cities, but we should be aware that Milan and Bologna are not wholly comparable, even though they both are called cities and they both have airports. To establish this comparability we need to enumerate characteristics within a reasonable range. "Reasonableness" is, of course, a judgment we make, but we can offer a strong defense to the extent that we have been systematic in reaching that judgment—that is, to the extent that we can enumerate demonstrably important criteria. (For example, Milan's airports are international and intercontinental and serve a population in the millions; Bologna's airport is principally domestic and serves a much smaller public.)

Comparability, at both the subjective and objective levels, is not fixed. In theory anything can be compared, but like rocks and pears, the broader the category, the more abstract the comparison. And the more abstract the comparison, the more superficial the insight is likely to be. Different data lead to different questions, and these differences may multiply within categories in such a way as to render the comparison across categories senseless. Although we must not make data "fit" our hypothesis or our commitment to compare, we must nevertheless be prepared to pursue, item for item, problems of comparability. To this end we will now consider some of the practical problems associated with the pursuit of comparative research.

Maintaining Comparability

There are several prerequisites to maintaining comparability in research. First, the subject must define a universe that has a corresponding and measurable object. Thus, from "Can urban planning improve the plight of our cities?" must flow the choice of particular cities and particular urban plans or possible plans. Second, the objects being compared ought to have both geographic and intellectual proximity. Let us consider the notion of intellectual proximity first.

All cities have something in common, and the ills of all cities may be subject to similar cures. But the research necessary to demonstrate the crucial common features of all cities—those located in all countries and cultures—has not yet been done. Hence, although cities may all be somewhat alike, the proposition is as yet hypothetical. Moreover, the greater the intellectual distance—as would be found, say, by comparing Paris with Lagos—the greater the number of variables that may intervene to disrupt the appreciation of possible causal relations. Cities may be set in environments so different as to render them, in fact, incomparable. Water, for example, may be a problem for all people in all human communities. Yet David Bradley and Gilbert and Anne White show vividly in their remarkable study *Drawers of Water* that the problem in East Africa is of so much greater a scale than in the advanced industrial world that the very concept of water as understood in New York is utterly different from the concept in Kenya.[7]

Of the old notion of "compare and contrast," we should remember that we are trying, first, to compare. The contrast may bring the concept into bold relief, but the comparison is more likely to deepen any insight. Thus, it is probably preferable to choose objects that fall within plainly similar universes. It may be that the results of the research that follows will yield greater possibility for comparing previously thought noncomparables, but it is probably best to start in the center of some circle and move concentrically outward. Put simply, the research task will probably be more fruitful if the researcher compares cities within the advanced industrial world or within the Third World, rather than comparing between the two.[8] Eventually, sensible comparabilities may be found between the two, but if experience in comparative social science research so far is any guide, that "eventually" is not yet with us.

Intellectual distance involves intellectual problems— problems concerned with the identification of criteria and the purpose of study. Geographical distance involves more practical problems. Comparing manpower policy in the United States and China might prove fascinating, but what chance is there that we will be able to shuttle like Henry Kissinger between Washington and Peking? I use the word "shuttle" because, as we will see in a moment, comparative research does not work best by examining single cases one after another.

There are only two possible solutions for comparing objects separated by significant geographic distances. One solution involves finding a reliable colleague with like interests who will run the same tests, seek the same data, stay in constant communication, and perform the research at approximately the same time. These conditions will be explained in a moment. The other solution requires money and time. The old maxim "If you want something done, do it yourself" is as true for research as for other things in life. Team research is exhilarating but difficult and often aggravating. On the other hand, the scale and scope of much comparative research requires it. When undertaking ambitious projects alone, especially over great physical distances, there is no substitute for money and time. Perseverance, dedication, commitment—none is enough.

It is fundamental to research that all paths of inquiry are not predictable. The scholar needs to be prepared to travel down whatever path beckons with the most promise. But what happens when in, say, Boston, we discover while pursuing an urban planning problem that, as Jane Jacobs suggests,[9] government—not planning—is central to improving the plight of our cities? Suppose we are comparing Boston with Montreal. In Montreal we might find that wherever planning was comprehensive, the outcome—on our scale of habitability—was preferable to outcomes where planning was less apparent. Then, in Boston, we find that the questions asked in Montreal are no longer the most pertinent. Do we conclude that planning makes a difference in Montreal but not in Boston and leave it at that? Or should we pursue the new line of inquiry in Boston and then return to Montreal to test it? In other words, do we maximize the original advantage of comparative research? Comparative research, you will recall, has the particular advantage of providing standards for testing hypotheses. When we tested the Montreal findings in Boston, some of them were denied and another hypothesis was suggested. Must we not return to Montreal to test the Boston findings?

This line of questioning opens up another central problem of comparative research. Do we look particularly for what is similar or for what is different? What is it we are really trying to learn? The answers to these questions must, again, be highly personal. Much of comparative research has been dedicated to demonstrating the "family of man"—demonstrating that we are "all in the same boat" with similar problems subject to similar solutions. But anthropologists, especially, have shown that the incredible variety of human culture distinguishes problems and solutions. In areas of East Africa, demands might be satisfied by the simple availability of clean water. In New York, however, such demands would also require that the clean water be no further away than the kitchen or bathroom tap. A pool of clean and available water in Central Park simply would not be an adequate solution for New Yorkers. Differences are great enough to warrant hope for the discovery of the range of possible preferences rather than a single answer. The range of human experience and preference informs us of possibility, whereas commonality suggests a certain inevitability. To the extent that we study social science in the belief that human choices matter, we must necessarily be inclined to explore differences before similarities.

Here there is a persistent tension that stalks all comparative social science research. The problem is that the objects of analysis must be similar enough to remain within the same universe of discourse, yet different enough to warrant thorough investigation. Furthermore, as we explore for differences we must constantly be sure that everything remains reasonably similar. There is the potential for a dilemma here, but really the matter is more a tension than a dilemma.

There can be little doubt that if we are to benefit from the comparative method in our study of Boston and Montreal, we will have to return to Montreal. Furthermore, we must be prepared to shuttle between the two places and test changing hypotheses. This shuttling proposition can sometimes be resolved through team research, but the range of cooperation must be very great. Whether shuttling or working as a team, researchers must recognize that the need to retest may result not only from changes in the overall hypotheses, but also from less dramatic differences in evidence in one or the other place that support or deny the hypothesis. When the smaller pieces of evidence vary, the maintenance of comparability becomes the most difficult of all.

Suppose we hypothesize that perception is crucial to the habitability of a city and that, therefore, people's responses to the survey question "Do you like living in this city?" will suggest whether the city is more or less habitable. Suppose, further, that in Montreal, across all manner of people on a first run of the survey, we receive positive responses. Then, in Boston, rich people seem to respond positively and poor people seem to respond negatively. In Montreal we did not sample systematically between rich and poor, nor did we in Boston. It was only after a quantity of negative responses in Boston that we detected a relationship between these responses and other characteristics. Now we are obliged to test systematically—in both cities—whether the correlation holds. The consequence is another trip—more money and more time. The alternative is a faulted hypothesis. Yet this matter of perception may be one of many indicators we are testing. In that case, we may save up a number of discrepancies and return to Montreal with all of them at the same time. Nevertheless, discrepancies—variations on the hypotheses between objects—may not always appear in different categories— or with respect to different variables—at the same time. We cannot count on one return trip to check out everything. As a line of inquiry develops we must check it out at our other site for guidance as to which direction might be pursued.

This need crosses all the research materials. If we seek, for example, to know about expropriation and changes in land value, we may consult transfers of land titles and deeds in a U.S. county office. When we ask for the same documents in provincial offices in Italy, we may learn that there are no comparable documents, but that through other materials we can collect other information about the land. We must then return to the county offices—or ask our research partner to return to the counties—to see if the kind of material in Italy can be matched in the United States. Documents will vary. What people say will vary. Furthermore, events in one place may influence events in another, which means that the *time* when questions are asked may be pertinent to when they are asked in another place.

Consider, for example, an inquiry of airport officials in Rome that reveals no concern at all for problems of noise. As we complete our inquiry, a special report is released by an investigating committee of the International Civil Aviation Organization (ICAO) concluding that noise is the most urgent problem on the airport agenda. We arrive in Milan to ask airport officials the same questions we asked in Rome. In Milan we find strong expressions of concern for problems of noise. Are these expressions of concern a consequence of greater awareness and sensitivity among officials in Milan or a consequence of the ICAO report? We will probably never know for sure. Had we been able to be in both Milan and Rome at the same time asking the same questions of comparable officials, the problem would have been less likely to occur. Being in two places at once means being two people—a feat that can be accomplished only by a research team. If the cases must be examined in series, the chances of variables intervening necessarily increase. The Rome-Milan problem might not have proved insoluble for the independent researcher, who may have turned to other sources in the historical record to establish whether there had been concern in Milan prior to the ICAO report. Our independent researcher may or may not have found other suitable documents, however. Even if he had, he still had to work harder to achieve like results.

Such a shuttle assumes that we, as comparative researchers, have a high tolerance for unstable existences. For the duration of a research project we must be prepared to move with some regularity between or among the objects we are analyzing. Our tolerance for such instability must therefore affect our choice of objects and, perhaps, our choice of subject as well.

In addition to being able to cope with this inescapable instability, we must be equipped with certain skills. Above all, if our objects are separated geographically, we must be equipped with appropriate language skills. Where the language is the same but the dialect or accent is different, we must also be sufficiently aware of cultural biases to overcome antagonisms we might unconsciously generate. If we speak Italian with a southern Italian accent, Milanese are not likely to take well to our inquiries about migrant labor, any more than a cultivated northern accent in Mississippi provokes sympathetic or helpful answers to questions about integration. Language can be a total barrier to the successful conduct of any research, but especially to the conduct of comparative research, where frequently more than one accent, dialect, or language is needed. The language problem can often be assuaged by deliberate cultural integration into the environment where the object of analysis is set, however. This approach requires personal skills of adaptability and sociability that must be sensed more than consciously taught or learned. No one can educate us to be natives if we are not born natives. Still, if we want Romans to give us honest answers, we might try following the oldest of maxims as much as possible: "When in Rome, do as the Romans do." Reduce the visibility of obviously conspicuous tasks, and try not to call inordinate attention to the inquiry.

Summing Up

Let us review briefly the key points we have considered thus far. The definition of a subject involves the recognition and choice of object(s). Whether the choice of a research topic begins conceptually with a subjective question or pragmatically with an object, every subject must be given an organizing framework, and every organizing framework must have examples. It is probably more efficient to choose the subject of research first, since this choice dictates the direction the inquiry will follow. In any event, subject and object must be seen together. Furthermore, the best place to begin the choice of object lies within the terms of our subjective question.

Subjects and objects imply hypotheses and models that, in turn, require testing. "If A then B" must be considered in light of all possible explanations: Although B might follow from A, it might also follow from C. Or it might follow from A in only some cases or under certain conditions. To find out whether B alone follows from A and whether it follows only from A, we must compare "If A then B" with, for example, "if C then B." And if we want to know whether A is "better" than B, we must compare them by applying identical criteria for each.

We test our hypotheses, therefore, through the establishment of norms and through comparison. The central dispute among people who do comparative social science research is whether comparison should be between highly similar or highly dissimilar objects. The preference depends on the purpose of research. Most comparative researchers now seem to seek the demonstration of similarity, whereas we are suggesting here that similar objects need to be chosen but ought to be employed for arraying choice and variety. Thus, the intellectual distance between objects must be sufficiently similar to impart like meaning to like questions, but the inquiry should seek to array the variety and scope within those common terms. Geography may also be a great impediment to our choices for comparison, for access to the objects of research is fundamental.

Finally, we have noted that comparative research requires certain skills, especially linguistic skills, and we must be sure that we are equipped sufficiently before we set out. Other skills, such as sociability, also matter but are less subject to modification or immediate development. Perhaps we should let our choices of subject and object be guided by our personal estimates of what methods we can execute best, accounting for whether we like interviewing or observing (e.g., going to meetings), or whether we tend to get along better with some kinds of people than with others. This personal assessment needs to be taken quite seriously; it concerns a fixed factor that unlike other skills is not readily subject to alteration or improvement.

All analysis depends upon good description. Thus, the quality of our observations determines the potential quality of all research. Once questions are framed and skills assessed, we must pursue the methods that will assure accurate, thorough, and impartial description. Much criticism has been leveled at description in social science; nevertheless, there can be no useful analysis without it.

Notes

1. The answers to the Weston questions may be found in Theodore J. Lowi, Benjamin Ginsberg, Elliot J. Feldman, et al., *Poliscide* (New York: Macmillan, 1976).

2. Discussion of this question is in Elliot J. Feldman and Jerome Milch, *Technocracy vs. Democracy: The Politics of International Airports* (forthcoming from Auburn House).

3. See Elliot J. Feldman, "An Illusion of Power: Military Conscription as a Dilemma of Liberal Democracy in Great Britain, the United States and France" (Ph.D. diss., Massachusetts Institute of Technology, 1972).

4. See, in particular, Robert K. Merton, "The Bearing of Sociological Theory on Empirical Research," *Social Theory and Social Structure*, rev. ed. (Glencoe, Ill.: Free Press, 1957), pp. 95–99.

5. Results of the relevant study may be found in Elliot J. Feldman, *Airport Siting as a Problem of Policy and Participation in Technological Societies: The Case of Milano-Malpensa* (Cambridge, Mass., and Torino: Harvard University Center for International Affairs and Fondazione Luigi Einaudi, 1978).

6. Gabriel A. Almond and Sidney Verba, *The Civic Culture: Political Attitudes and Democracy in Five Nations* (Princeton, N.J.: Princeton University Press, 1963). See especially the survey provided in the appendix.

7. Gilbert F. White, David I. Bradley, and Anne V. White, *Drawers of Water: Domestic Water Use in East Africa* (Chicago: University of Chicago Press, 1972).

8. See discussion in Elliot J. Feldman, "Comparative Public Policy: Field or Method?" *Comparative Politics* (January 1978):289–293.

9. Jane Jacobs, *The Death and Life of Great American Cities* (New York: Random House, 1961).

2
Field Research Methods

There are *not* many ways to collect information for social science analysis. The laboratory where controlled experiments may be undertaken is, among social scientists, almost uniquely the domain of some psychologists. Most social scientists are denied a variety of experimental techniques. The attitudes, cognitions, perceptions, values, choices, and actions of people that concern us are not easily distilled or replicated and are certainly not likely agents for test-tube reactions. Moreover, since this book focuses on research that is neither psychological nor psychiatric, much observational data lie outside what we can use. We are not psychoanalyzing respondents. However sophisticated the techniques for data analysis may be, by and large, all social science techniques for data collection reduce themselves to what we see, what we hear, and what we read.[1]

Each of these means of collecting data suffers from a variety of important limitations. What we see, for example, is, in fact, only what we think or believe we see. Certainty depends on verification. We can increase certainty by collecting the testimony of witnesses, but we know from the eyewitness accounts of an accident, for example, how short of verification we can fall. If a book descends from my desk to the floor, I may say it fell; someone else may swear that I dropped it; another observer may say it was pushed over by accident. Moreover, not only does such testimony rely on what we and others think we see; it also depends on the honesty of the witnesses. How can we be certain witnesses have not conspired to deceive us? (Indeed, famous cognitive dissonance tests conducted by Muzafer Sherif at Columbia University revealed that the conspiracy of witnesses can be very effective in deceiving someone collecting testimony for verification.[2]) Thus, in trying to verify what we think or believe we see, hear, or read, we confront the problem of sufficiency. How much testimony, whether visual or aural, is enough? Is the legal guideline of one or two corroborative witnesses sufficient in social science? In any event, we must accept at the outset that we deal strictly in probabilities and that we are, in effect, never certain of anything. We can be no more certain than we are confident in the consistent reliability of our personal faculties. As imperfect beings, we are inevitably imperfect data gatherers.

Armed with the certainty that our data collection is inevitably imperfect, we must choose techniques that will (1) correspond in the tightest possible fit to the information we seek to gather; (2) maximize reliability; and (3) reduce error as much as humanly possible. All social science techniques for collecting data constitute sophisticated forms of seeing, hearing, and reading. These forms vary a great deal from one another, however. Perhaps the most important factor to consider in choosing among them is economy, in terms of both time and money (even when the two are not necessarily equivalent). Since we cannot read everything or talk to everyone, we must keep our study confined as much as possible to our chosen objects and we must try as scrupulously as possible to collect only information pertinent to our subject. Everything else is extraneous—a burden to collect, catalogue, and maintain. Being selective in what we collect and what we ask is one of the hardest of all research tasks. We should therefore be vigilant and remind ourselves constantly of just what our subject is as we examine the object. We must always remember why we are studying a particular object beyond any intrinsic interest suggested by the object itself. It is very easy—and very unfortunate—to waste time and energy.

Surveys

The survey[3] is perhaps, next to reading, the most popular yet least economical of social science field methods. Its popularity stems from several factors. (1) It appeals to our egalitarian instincts by permitting us to include many objects of potentially countless backgrounds and interests, while creating jobs when done on a mass basis. (Some social scientists may consider this last point insulting or irrelevant, but surveys have provided considerable employment for graduate students, and the function of surveys in this respect has not always been purely incidental.) (2) The survey permits us to gather quantities of similar data within fixed time periods. (3) The survey, if conducted in a sufficiently random way, can normally be replicated and therefore seems to simulate best the laboratory experiment. (4) The survey holds many variables constant simultaneously, which increases reliability. (5) Surveys can be at the same time fancy and fun. All these factors have contributed to the survey's unparalleled prominence in the methodology literature of sociology and political science. It also has been by far the most favored tool of comparative political scientists. But let us consider some disadvantages.

Surveys are expensive. It is necessary either to expend enormous amounts of personal time and energy or to employ others to ask the questions. For every person questioned, a separate form must be prepared. There must be a code to keep the data from different respondents classified in a common way. Without a code it is extremely difficult to compile the data. There must be mathematical computation, and if there are more than twenty people in the survey, a computer may be necessary to analyze the data. Computers and computer time are expensive.

Surveys are also not as reliable as they may at first seem. Although sufficiently large samples may compensate for error or deceit, every answer depends upon the respondent's interpretation of the question. The range of possible interpretations—and hence misunderstandings—is infinite. Not only might the language lead to misunderstanding, but an abundance of literature now reports that the questioner's unconscious biases often betray themselves in subtle ways to respondents. Respondents may answer with these biases in mind.[4]

Surveys can also be unreliable because they account for those who answer but say little or nothing about those who do not. Catching people on a street corner and asking, "Hey, could you answer a couple of questions?" might seem reasonably random, but it is impossible to know whether those who never have the minute to stop constitute a more important or coherent sample. Those who do stop may represent a population only of the "stoppers." But before going further in this general statement about surveys, let us systematically categorize the kinds of surveys and make more precise suggestions about each of them.

Demography Versus Attitudes

Broadly speaking there are two kinds of surveys—or, at least, there are two kinds of information that can be gathered in a survey. We can ask people for certain facts about them- selves—demographic questions—such as how old they are, where they live, or how much they earn. We can also ask people what they think, how they feel about something, or how they have behaved or might behave (as in voting); these are attitudi- nal questions. Some surveys are demographic, others are atti- tudinal, and, inevitably, some are both.

We should be aware that when we ask people for facts about themselves, the "facts" are not always clear. For one thing, peo- ple are not always ready to give away certain information. Con- ventional women may not reveal their correct age, and conven- tional men might not reveal their correct income. How often would a casual acquaintance answer your inquiry about their parents' income? Deception may be deliberate, or it may be completely accidental. And some simple facts may not be dis- cernible. For example, a tenant farmer may be perfectly cooper- ative but nonetheless unable to cite a cash figure for his income. Although he may receive some meager wage and live in a run- down shack, probing may reveal that he uses the shack free of charge, including the utilities, and that the owner's truck is at his disposal. He may also be able to hunt and fish on the land and, consequently, has an excellent diet without ever spending anything but his spare time to feed himself and his family. The rent, utilities, transportation, and food all come as fringe benefits, but surely must be regarded as income. A cash figure for his income, therefore, is elusive, even though he is sincere in his effort to satisfy our factual request.

If demographic data sometimes prove elusive, attitudinal data are normally available in abundance. Generally in surveys, if we ask a question we get an answer. Unfortunately, not every answer is meaningful. People have opinions on most subjects. We can try to test the reliability of attitudinal answers by asking the same question in different ways at different points in the survey, but the respondent may or may not prove consistent.

The difference between probing for demographic data and probing for attitudinal data involves a difference in purpose. In asking demographic questions, we have already defined some group and now want to describe it. That group may live in a certain geographic area, attend a certain school, church, function, or meeting, or share some other factor we identify. We begin by identifying something in common and then inquire whether that particular factor is related to others that are shared: Are the neighbors all middle class? Are they all approximately the same age? Are their families the same size? We might also ask more attitudinal questions: Do they have similar aspirations? Do they envision the world the same way? Are they concerned about the same issues? All these questions, whether demographic or attitudinal, arise after we have already identified some respondent group *as a group* that we then want to describe. In such instances we begin with a demographic inquiry.

When we begin with an attitudinal inquiry we tend to ask whether an apparently heterogeneous sample of people shares certain patterns of behavior or belief. Are there linkages or "bundles" of beliefs, and can we locate any variables that will predict others? For example, will people who profess a fervent belief in organized religion also profess a preference for the Republican party? Attitudinal and demographic information *may* prove highly related. Whatever the commitment to organized religion, for instance, rich people may prove more likely than poor people to support Republicanism. The point is, however, that our sample tends to be random and from it we seek to identify groups or clusters on the basis of attitudes or ideology. To identify such groups, we must have hypotheses, for they determine what questions we will ask.

Few surveys are either completely demographic or completely attitudinal—most combine the two kinds of information and, indeed, attempt to correlate between them. Nevertheless, we should note that the departure point for each type is different because of a basic difference in purpose.

Survey Methods

There may be only two basic kinds of information to be gathered in a survey, but there are several different approaches to collecting this information. Let us consider some of them.

There are four main ways in which a survey can be administered: (1) the survey can be mailed or left on the doorstep for people to fill in, and it can be returned by mail or picked up by the investigator; (2) it can be delivered to people to fill in while the researcher waits and perhaps helps; (3) the questions and format can be kept by the questioner who personally asks each question of the respondent; or (4) the survey can be conducted over the telephone. The relative advantages and disadvantages of these four methods depend largely on cost. Delivering the survey, leaving it for completion, and returning to collect it is certainly the cheapest method. It also eliminates variation in presentation. However, this method has certain unfortunate aspects. For one thing, it normally means that the survey results are not reliable for individuals but must be regarded more in terms of households. Husbands and wives—however much they may be asked not to—often will collaborate if they are at home together facing the same questions on separate forms. For another thing, there is usually a high level of unreturned forms, and there is simply no way of knowing—short of subsequent personal follow-up visits—who does not respond and why.

Remaining present while the respondents complete the survey involves a considerable sacrifice of time. It also can seriously inhibit the respondent, who may feel embarrassed or pressured and, hence, hurry to complete the form, hesitate to ask questions, or both. The personal administration of a survey is probably the best method, but it is not free of important disadvantages. Many people will refuse to talk with a stranger in their homes. Not only is interviewing in people's homes clearly the most expensive method, but it also places an enormous burden on the questioner, who must instill confidence in the respondent and pose each question in a clear and unambiguous manner.

The way in which the questioner dresses and talks can have a serious impact on the results. Jeans and T-shirts may provoke honest and useful responses in a university dormitory, but only hostility can be expected in response to such attire at a meeting of the board of trustees. If the sample is to be random on the sidewalk (or over the telephone or door-to-door through various neighborhoods), it may be extremely difficult to anticipate how to dress or how to talk. But, unfortunately, appearances and impressions count.

The telephone is used most frequently by national polling organizations and political candidates. When located within the community being sampled, the caller operates at the lowest telephone rates and eliminates all other travel costs. The telephone also enjoys the advantage of an impersonal interview, reducing the influence of appearances on results. But the time of day may define the sample: Working people will not be home most of the time, and evening calls frequently conflict with dinner hours. Many people will not want to spend time answering questions over the telephone, and it can be difficult to generate a reliable random sample. Overall, the telephone can be a cheap and desirable instrument for testing acquaintance with a product, but it is less reliable for lengthy inquiries or for defining a respondent group.

Open-ended and Closed Surveys

In addition to these four methods for conducting surveys, a survey may be open-ended or closed. That is, it may be loosely structured so that the researcher can ask different series of questions depending on the responses given, or it may have a fixed set of items allowing for a specified range of answers. It is possible to alternate between these two types if the survey is administered personally, but basically, open-ended surveys are administered personally, and closed surveys do not require such personal attention.

A closed survey assumes not only that the questions to be asked are the same for everyone but also that all questions will be asked and understood in the same way. The phrasing of a question can alter its meaning or can alter the understanding conveyed to different respondents. Avoidance of errors attributable to this kind of misunderstanding depends upon consistent phrasing. As we will mention in Chapter 3, it is often necessary to "probe" for answers, even on closed surveys. Nevertheless, the principal feature and value of the closed format is its relative assurance of consistency in the phrasing and presentation of questions.

Scaling and Coding

Whether the survey is open or closed also affects how it is scaled or coded. Scaling and coding are necessary for the storage and retrieval of information. If we merely write down whatever we are told, we will face a wealth of disorganized prose defying later analysis. Unfortunately, the precise way in which people say things is often much more accurate and honest than the categories into which we might force their answers to suit our purposes. For example, suppose we ask a woman if she buys eggs at the supermarket. We have coded her possible responses as $1 = yes$, $2 = no$, and $3 = sometimes$. She might answer that she used to, doesn't at present, but will again as soon as the supermarket fulfills its promise to improve the quality of its eggs. Her answer is not "yes," because she does not at present purchase her eggs at the supermarket; her answer is not really "no," because she used to make such purchases and will again soon—only at this moment is "no" accurate; nor does "sometimes" correspond to what we have been told, since at present the answer is "no." For the purpose of computer analysis, we are asking all our questions on the basis of three possible answers: 1, 2, and 3. (The computer analysis will match the 1's, 2's, and 3's and thereby indicate clusters.) But all answers do not always suit our coding, and we have therefore thrown out numerous answers unwittingly.

Similarly, we might scale answers. For example, we might ask, "On a scale of 1 to 10—1 being terrible and 10 being wonderful—how do you rate this course?" On this particular item the respondent might say, "This course is fragmented: the readings rate a 10, but the lectures rate only a 1." Perhaps the survey offers separate items for the readings and the lectures, but if it does not, shall we conclude that the course is rated "5" or "10" or "1"? Consider whether you have ever seen a course evaluation form that did justice to what you wanted to convey about the subject and the professor. Both coding and scaling normally require us to increase the number of discrete items to heighten detail. However, shades of difference in items may not always be apparent to respondents. Furthermore, the amount of time a respondent is prepared to devote to a survey is limited, and a point can be reached rather quickly after which there are either no answers or the answers are capricious. The respondent may be pleased to have as many discrete items as possible when trying to find a love-match by computer but may be somewhat less disposed to answer a like number of items concerning his shopping habits.

Hence, there are advantages and disadvantages to various kinds of scaling and coding that depend, above all, on the purpose of the survey. Some scaling or coding is inescapable. But we should take this particular problem one step further: When preparing a survey, we should ask ourselves repeatedly not only about the purpose of the whole survey but about the purpose of each item as well. We should ask ourselves, "If we have an answer to this question, what will we then know or be able to deduce?" If we are unable to specify the value of any given question, it should be excluded from the survey. Surveys often begin with questions (or observations) about age, sex, profession, and income; yet, this (and other "standard") information frequently proves unrelated to the survey's objective. For each such piece of information it is essential to have a hypothesis (e.g., if any group supports a military draft, it will be the people over draft-eligible age). Coding then should be adjusted to the hypothesis. If the hypothesis involves bracketing respondents into two main age groups—those within and those above draft-eligible age—then specific ages need not be recorded and can only add time and expense to later analysis.

Every survey, if at all possible, should be pretested for the value of each item: the phrasing, and order of questions; and the overall format and length. Pretesting—practicing with the survey on a small number of people—should guide us to eliminate some items and to include others, to alter scaling or coding to allow for answers in fact given, to alter the order of questions, to restate items that apparently are not clear, and to lengthen or shorten the entire survey.

Choosing Populations

In preparing a survey, then, we must specify our purpose and check each item for its phrasing, for the specific information it can provide, and for its contribution to the overall purpose. We must establish a format that is easy to follow, clear, and precise. We must set down questions in a logical order, especially where some questions depend upon prior answers. We must try to be both brief and complete. And, finally, we must decide who will answer these questions—that is, we must choose a population.

The choice of population depends, of course, on our purpose. If we want to know whether airport neighbors are economically and socially homogeneous, we have to ask people who live near airports about their economic and social situations. If we want to know whether Italians are likely to vote more for the Communist party in the next general election, we need to draw a sample from all of Italy. What we are trying to find out determines whom we ask, but there is also a quantitative problem: How many members of the relevant population do we question? Do we examine all of the population? Some fixed percentage? If we cannot reach an entire population, then we need a random sample. There is disagreement as to how many people constitute a sufficient statistical sample, with the minimum number in steady decline despite the "law of large numbers," which promises greater statistical validity with bigger samples. Some social scientists have even suggested that samples of less than one hundred are reliable.[5]

Although it may be true that it is quite enough to survey fewer than one hundred people of a given population, we must be very careful about how we draw our sample. If, for example, our target group is airport neighbors, it may be important to know that several different legal districts border the airport. These districts may have different zoning ordinances that in turn govern whether rich or poor people are likely to be found in a given district. Suppose, moreover, that these districts tend to be ethnically exclusive and that the last names of people in these ethnic groups cluster around different letters in the alphabet. We randomly open a telephone book (which is consolidated for all these districts) and choose every tenth name to draw a sample of, say, twenty-five people. We subsequently may discover, much to our dismay, that we are interviewing twenty-five people from the same ethnic group and from the same neighborhood—hardly a representative sample of airport neighbors.

This set of unusual conditions may seem somewhat contrived. Nonetheless, it should warn us that randomizing may require being aware of numerous conditions first. In this instance, we may have to avoid the telephone book and randomize by street addresses. Once we overcome the peculiar conditions of a given case, we may then draw a random sample.

Drawing the random (or stratified random) sample does not complete the task. Suppose we generate responses from only ten of our set of twenty-five? (Fifteen may not return the survey forms, may hang up the telephone or not answer, may not be home, or may slam the door in our faces.) Ten people do not a survey make. We will have to try again. For this reason another rule of thumb is that an initial sample should be at least one-third to one-half larger than necessary. Experience shows that in a normal survey one-third to one-half of the drawn sample will not provide responses for whatever reason. This percentage, furthermore, may vary depending on the manner in which the survey is administered. Percentages are better for personally administered questionnaires, worse for forms put in the mail. Financial inducements, follow-up, and high-status sponsorship all may increase the return, but each adds to the time and expense involved. It is best not to sample at all, but rather to aim for the whole population. Obviously, a 100 percent response reduces sampling error. Unfortunately, such an aim is rarely practical.

Administering the Questions

Besides drawing the sample, there is the problem of who will administer the questions. It is normally best to do it ourselves. We know better than anyone what we are trying to find out, what we are really asking, and what we really mean by a given question. If we seek a large number of people (whether aiming for 100 percent of the village expropriated for an atomic accelerator or surveying Italians on their voting preferences), we must find others to ask some questions on our behalf. In this case it is important that we find people who (1) speak the language of the respondents; (2) know enough about the respondent population to know how to dress and present themselves inoffensively (miniskirted women should not administer questionnaires in Palermo); (3) are familiar with the survey, its purpose, and its content; and (4) have practiced—either with this survey or with others—asking questions and recording answers. This last item of training is especially important if those who conduct the survey are expected to code or scale while administering the questionnaire.

Summary

We have now treated—however briefly—most of the ways in which surveys are administered and questions are posed. We should remember, however, that for all the survey's attractions it is expensive and time-consuming. Its purpose must be very clearly defined, or its payoff will not be at all commensurate with its costs. It is important in all social science research to ask a fair number of people basically the same questions, but the systematic survey is not always the best way to accomplish the objective. Let us remember finally that in comparative research, all of the different populations under investigation must be asked the same questions, and requirements of randomization, sampling, and method of administration must apply equally to each population as if it were an entirely separate undertaking.

Let us turn now to some of the other ways in which we can collect information—in particular, to elite interviewing and documentary collection and analysis, both of which will be discussed again in Chapter 3.

Elite Interviews

By elite or "in-depth" interviewing, we do not mean asking questions only of heads of state, corporation executives, or the like. We mean any elite within a given culture or subculture.

Thus, we might be talking to heads of state, but we might also be talking to tribal leaders or the directors of the local Boys Club or YMCA. The elite is comprised of the leaders or decision makers, whatever they are leading and whatever they are making decisions about. But we must make our distinctions finer to appreciate fully that mass surveys are not the same as elite interviews.

The central difference between the survey and the elite interview is the purpose of each interview and the technique employed. Although many of the same questions must be put to different people in a designated elite, *no two interviews are exactly alike.* This is so because each person has been deliberately, not randomly, chosen. We do not seek a sample of a population. We seek sworn testimony from as much of a particular population as we can reach.

In the early 1960s Daniel Lerner and Morton Gordon ran a mass survey of European elites.[6] They asked leaders, decision makers, civil servants, and businessmen—so-called opinion makers—the same set of questions in closed interviews. Their population was chosen on the basis of reputation and apparent social, political, and economic importance. They surveyed attitudes and opinions on a wide variety of subjects related to the development of Europe. In terms of our definitions, Lerner and Gordon conducted a mass survey, not elite interviews.

Every member of an elite plays (or has played) a unique role in the set of events or decisions we are studying. We choose the people we see to learn as much as possible about that role—in order to understand as much as possible about the entire process of decision making or about the entire set of events. Thus, elite interviewing is always conducted in part for information that we cannot find written down somewhere—information that only members of an elite seem to know.

There is also a second, often more important, purpose in elite interviewing. Elites have certain perspectives, sometimes shared, sometimes in conflict. Decisions are sometimes consensual and sometimes strife-torn. People we might have assumed were important may have played no role, while others we had discounted may have been crucial. We need to see enough people to establish who was involved and who was not, what roles were played, and what positions were taken. But above all, perhaps, we want to know something about the perceptions of the decision makers or leaders. That is, we want to find out what each of them thought they were or are doing, what motives each defines, what general views are shared or in conflict. In this area—the perceptual area of our inquiry—elites should be subjected to the same questions, in contrast to the informational part of our inquiry, which focused on the uniqueness of each role player. However, even in this stage, there are still important differences between this method and the survey.

Elite interviews must be open-ended, and the structure must be flexible. Although we may plan to ask our questions according to a certain priority, we must be prepared to pursue them in the order the respondents perceive pertinent. The respondents may be prepared to answer all our questions, but they might think the tenth item on our list second in importance. As they speak, without ever seeing our list, they may skip to that item. On the one hand, we must be flexible enough to follow. On the other, we must be firm enough to cover the ground we deem most important before the respondent meanders into other subject areas and then terminates the interview.

Elite interviews also afford an opportunity to hear more than one version of the same story. The technique of storytelling is common to psychological interviewing; the difference here is that we know much of the story must correspond to some event generally perceived as having happened. The psychological interviewer is likely to amass a good deal more fiction than fact from a respondent. Each elite version of a given set of events or decisions will yield peculiar and important perspectives and perceptions.

For the sake of nomenclature, I should explain here that indepth, open-ended interviewing with a precisely chosen set of people (for example, all the people who participated directly in the decision to invade the Suez Canal) will involve most of the same methods as elite interviewing. We might have to go about arranging interviews differently—a subject we will take up in Chapter 3—but the actual conduct of the interview and the range of things we might want to find out are probably similar.

A unique population group—which we identify as unique and as a group *before* we conduct interviews—will, for the sake of our terminology here, constitute an elite.

Summing Up and
Reflecting on Elite Interviews

Elite interviews, then, involve a specific group of people, require open-ended and flexible inquiry, and are likely to involve both informational and perceptual components. Furthermore, elite interviewing does not normally allow for sampling. Rather, the object is to reach as many people as possible who are identified as part of the group. Constraints of time, money, or language may prevent our conducting all elite interviews ourselves (or, for that matter, conducting any of them personally in a question-answer session). But let us be candid: In studying an elite—especially one with a story to tell—there is no substitute for face-to-face meetings.

Elite interviews have a number of obvious advantages over other research methods. Besides offering an "inside" story and an "inside" perspective, they often provide vital information. These apparent advantages should not be overstated, however. Elite interviews are expensive. They may not require the manpower of a survey, and they may not involve the computer or complex statistical compilation, but they do involve quantities of time. We will discuss in Chapter 4 some of the more specific constraints and time demands. Let it suffice here to note that at least two hours must be allowed for an elite interview, including travel and waiting time. As the research advances, interviews will last longer, even when the value of the extra information begins to diminish. Since we might be able to read anywhere from fifty to one hundred pages of documents, books, or articles during two hours, we should be sure to ask ourselves before conducting an elite interview whether the chosen respondent is apt to contribute enough to merit time that might be better spent reading. It is often true that matters become clearer to us when we learn them in conversation or discussion, but if particular information is already written down and we have not taken the trouble to find or read it, we may be wasting our own time and the respondent's.

We should be aware, furthermore, that the more we know about a given problem the more marginal the return on elite interviews is likely to be. Finally, we should be conscious that elites may be scattered geographically. If we propose to see them, we may have to travel great distances. While it is usually easier to arrange to see people whose roles were played in the past, those currently active are likely to dwell in one geographic area. People out of power or responsibility or who are no longer unique, though more receptive, are also more likely to be dispersed. The trade-off on our time and resources in this choice should not be taken lightly. During World War II every American citizen was urged to ask when driving—in the name of resource conservation—"Is this trip necessary?" We should ask ourselves a similar question in preparing and conducting elite interviews.

Documentary Research

Interviewing, whether as survey or as open-ended elite inquiry, is almost always the most enjoyable part of social science research. It has a certain sense of adventure and challenge that is not common to other research methods. However, there is an almost inescapable pleasure/pain principle in social science research, meaning that we often have to endure a considerable amount of pain before we ever get to the pleasure of interviewing. It is not so much that other research tasks are painful. Rather, it is that their productivity is not always apparent to us. They can also be isolating, even alienating, and they can be tedious. But for all that, they cannot be avoided.

The "they" to which I am referring involves the collection and examination of written materials. These materials may be found in library books, government releases, public statements, personal papers, official documents, archives, and newspapers. There is no substitute in this task for a good and complete library, but it is highly unlikely that any single library will contain all the materials pertinent to a study. We must go out and look for materials—from both private individuals and from institutions—and we must keep in mind some of the problems that frequently haunt a researcher.

Common Research Fears

A researcher can probably never know when everything pertinent, such as papers, reports, and other studies, has been found. There is always the worry that somewhere someone is doing the very same thing—writing the very same story—and better. Whereas this worry cannot be discounted, it ought not to be inflated either. When two people are engaged in the same research, the probability of their crossing paths is extremely great. Furthermore, it may be attributable simply to the wonders of man, but when we have a problem or a question that we have a burning incentive to explore, the probability that someone else has precisely the same problem or question— framed precisely the same way—is almost negligible. Even the most obvious and apparently vital subjects often constitute virgin research ground. Some aspect of what we are doing might suddenly appear elsewhere, but it is not likely to overtake our whole project.

A similar fear is that what we are doing has already been done. This worry haunts the historian far more than the student in comparative social science. Indeed, the student of contemporary problems may hope fervently that all the background to the present subject already has been assembled. However, before embarking full throttle on a piece of research, we must do substantial preliminary inquiry. We should begin with the recognized scholars and experts in the field. If we do not know who they are, we should go to a library and find out who has written on our subject and on related subjects. We should examine the books in the field. We should examine the bibliographies. The University of Michigan maintains an almost complete collection of doctoral dissertations and can report on research in given fields and subject areas. Government agencies, such as the National Academy of Science, maintain lists of work in progress, and there are several services that publish abstracts of major journal articles. We can also ask scholars and experts (including journalists) whether they know of any work that preempts our plans.

These preliminary studies and inquiries narrow considerably the likelihood that we will fall midway into our research onto our whole study already done by someone else. It is not impossible that we will discover ourselves replicating other work, therein making no new contribution, but the probability of doing so is very small.

A researcher is also haunted by the possibility that all of his other research may depend completely on one unavailable document, record, report, or testimony. Good research opens enough avenues, asks enough challenging questions, and relies on a sufficient diversity of sources to escape such a problem entirely. Every piece of research does not answer every question raised, and this or that unavailable piece of information may hold the answer to a particular question. Nevertheless, good research raises more than one question, and there is always more than one way to get at least an approximate answer. We might not be able to state what Neville Chamberlain's intentions were without Neville Chamberlain's papers, but does it matter? The testimony of others interpreting Chamberlain's motives surely reveals the important historical data, for the explanation of the behavior of actors in the international arena lies in what the actors perceived in each other. Chamberlain may have been misunderstood. What is more important is how he was understood by others and how, consequently, they behaved. His papers may help us apologize for him, but they probably will not help us much in our social science understandings. They may be nice to have, but they should never be crucial or decisive. We began, after all, by suggesting that the greatest certainty in our inquiries is uncertainty. No single piece of information or set of materials can provide us with certainty. We must have other materials in order to make a case.

Another, and even more compelling, research fear is that one will find not too little, but rather too much. As in the task of interviewing, we must constantly try to stay focused on what we are asking and on what we are trying to find out. It is unnerving that apparently extraneous materials often prove pertinent long after we had been inclined to discard them. This tendency leads us to collect a great deal that does, indeed, prove extraneous. There is no convenient rule to follow in this matter, but there is something we can try always to remember: whatever we collect we will have to analyze. Data may be nice to have, but we need only consider the quantities of data collected, stored, and ignored by government bureaucracies everywhere to appreciate that data are important only when they are analyzed. We should attempt, therefore, to confine our collection to what we have some reason—however vague—to believe we can and indeed eventually will use. Our research involves becoming expert in something. Hence, we may try to read everything on the subject. In some instances, so little will have been said or written or analyzed as to make this objective perfectly feasible. However, more often this objective will be impossible. Consequently, we need to emphasize again the importance of selectivity. We must husband our time as our most valuable resource.

Sources of Information

An important thing to remember about documentary research is that valuable data may be in unlikely places. Political scientists, for example, rarely begin where they should: by reading statutes. Laws define the tasks of agencies, the values of societies, the rules of behavior. They constitute the norm against which performance in a given sphere can be measured. One of the first tasks of a political scientist, therefore, should be a visit to a law library to read exactly what rules govern the phenomena under investigation.

Students of political science should also read the debates of the law makers. What a congressman has done in voting for a law and what he *thinks* he is doing when he casts his vote often offer a fascinating study in contrasts. Reading debates affords us the opportunity to consider what objectives and goals are on the agenda or what the society or the government is at least trying to accomplish. Similarly, since many of the laws have been refined or redefined by the courts, court decisions are an important resource for understanding competing views of law and the prevailing view of interpretation at any given point in time. Court decisions are an invaluable resource for learning about social conflict and social and political rules.

Other information sources include statements and reports from government agencies. The army, for example, might sponsor a law to appropriate money for a new weapon. What has the army said on the matter? What studies did it conduct? What evidence or information did the army submit to the law makers? Answers to these questions will be found in the official record. The army's press officer or public relations officer may provide them; the newspapers may report them; and the records of the law makers may display them. They constitute documents.

Governments and private agencies also frequently hire consultants. Consultants write reports that often can be made available and often include raw data, analysis, and recommendations. Whether in a study for building a dam (of value to geographers) or a weapon (of interest to economists and political scientists), the consultants' efforts can be of great value in research. Remember, however, that agencies we might not expect to deal with certain subjects sometimes do. The Bureau of the Census in the United States, for example, maintains excellent documents on housing. We need to investigate the less than obvious offices.

Scholars are often unjustifiably critical of newspapers. Newspapers constitute a daily record, however, and while the stories may be superficial or incomplete, much basic information will be found there. Moreover, newspapers over time can prove surprisingly thorough. Little news emerged, for example, from the publication of the Pentagon papers. Albeit piecemeal, the newspapers had already carried most of the stories. Inadvertently, journalists constitute a worldwide research team whose data collection may serve social science analysis. The scholar who rejects this source may affect superiority but is ultimately foolish. Sometimes a story may not be carried, but a journalist may be willing to share copy. The newspapers of record—like the *New York Times, Toronto Globe and Mail, Le Monde*, the *London Times*—and journalists' notes are fundamental documents.

Institutes and libraries may provide special services that make available materials otherwise difficult to use. Not only do some libraries and archives maintain special collections and private papers, but the Royal Institute for International Affairs in London, for example, maintains a press library of cut, catalogued, and cross-referenced newspaper stories from all over the world. The collection, though suffering from certain biases and gaps, is peerless in its breadth, depth, range of time treated (since World

War I), and efficiency. The Council on Foreign Relations in New York and the International Institute for Strategic Studies in London also offer press services (though not nearly as comprehensive and for subjects sometimes more narrowly defined). Newspapers themselves, furthermore, often keep their stories organized, as in the *Times'* yearly index. Newspaper compilation of this kind can save considerable time over reading the daily paper for periods of several months or years. Shortcuts such as organized press collections are not always available, especially in some fields. Nevertheless, it is useful always to explore for them before embarking on some endeavors ourselves.

In every instance where institutions are involved there are institutional records. They may not always be immediately accessible, but more often than not perseverance will produce them. If we are interested in the socioeconomic composition of airport users, it may pay to ask the airport authorities if they have collected such data before rushing off to run a survey. That step would be normal in data collection. But we might also discover an institute specializing in air transportation or in market research that has also undertaken this area of concern. Political parties often maintain files on a host of nonpolitical issues and also have official positions available from the party headquarters. Furthermore, consumer organizations collect data on all sorts of products and services.

In short, the directly responsible agencies and parties may not be the sole sources of data. Field research should be empirical, which means it results not only from collecting new data but also from exploiting data collected by others. Such data often may be found in organization offices, special institutes and libraries. Established scholars and journalists will frequently know of these sources, and they should be asked.

We should remember that many officials have private papers or personal libraries which, on request, they may share with us. These constitute an invaluable documentary resource. Sometimes it will be necessary to request access in writing; it is preferable to ask personally at an interview. Either way, we should not forget the possibility that such papers may exist and that we may be allowed to use them. When documents are offered, especially during an interview, we should never fail to accept them, even if at first we doubt their value. Later on, they may surprise us in their usefulness. And when respondents have mailing lists for the release of documents, we should sign up.

There are other kinds of documentary information readily available. The mass public registers its general tendencies on issues in only one way—voting. We must be very wary of voting data, for, as we have said before, we never know *why* people vote as they do. But voting data can tell us whether change is occurring. Voting data can serve admirably both as a barometer and as a thermometer of society. The more people vote, the higher the passions, and whether voting is stable or changing is an important storm gauge.

Much social science methodology concerns statistical measures. Statistics are not the product solely of government studies or reports, however, nor must a researcher conduct a survey or rely on someone else's. There are many ways other than surveys to gather statistics, and the most imaginative tend to be the most successful. Anything that can be counted can also be calculated, graphed, compared.

The Risks of Using Events Data

Many social scientists rely on what they call "events data." Such data are used in quantitative analyses for measuring indicators and testing hypotheses. Events data usually are derived from newspapers, magazines, and journals. They record an event. For example, one might scour the *New York Times* for reports on strikes and then add up the number of occasions when a strike has occurred. Newspapers might also be the source of counting incidents of violence, whether in individual crime or in riots or mob behavior.

Using these data is risky. We are obliged to depend on the observations of others, particularly journalists, who may have a particular point of view or a need to report something a particular way. A sensational press might report a peaceful demonstration as violent, or a crowd of angry people as a riot. A pro-government newspaper might estimate a crowd of 100,000 demonstrators as nearer to 25,000, which seemed to happen often during the early days of anti–Vietnam War protest. We compound such misleading reporting when we aggregate the inaccuracies. We might also misinterpret across different national experiences. A strike in Italy may last only a few hours and be motivated politically, whereas a strike in the United States may last months but be concerned only with the size of a paycheck. The intent and character of each is different, but both are called "strikes" and to the untrained or ethnocentric observer they may appear similar.

We must remember, then, that the analysis of data can be only as good as the data themselves. The value of the data, in turn, depends on the quality of observation. Events data represent the compilation of observations, usually from the perspective of others; they must be treated accordingly.

Visual Techniques of Data Collection

We listen to answers in interviews, and we read the documentary record. We can also see. If we want to know how often the municipal government cleans streets in different neighborhoods, there are three possible ways to find out: (1) we can ask municipal officials; (2) we can ask residents of the neighborhoods; and (3) we can visit the neighborhoods and see for ourselves. Does a neighborhood still change rapidly under ethnic pressure? Perhaps the best and easiest way to answer the question is to cruise the streets counting "For Sale" signs.

There is a great deal we can observe outside the laboratory without asking questions or reading documents. The meaning we impart to what we observe visually is no less valid than what we observe aurally, and it is much less obtrusive. However, we often have to be imaginative in developing useful indicators. For example, one indicator of the wealth of a neighborhood or community may be the percentage of new automobiles in front of homes. Or perhaps we can count the number of garages built for more than one car. The number of different doorbells on a building may tell us how many families reside inside, and we can see for ourselves the size of the building.

Visual techniques are especially valuable in community or neighborhood research. They are obviously less valuable in studying, for example, bureaucratic decision making, but observing the books and documents on desks and shelves in offices where we may be interviewing can give us useful clues to relevant data. We should always remember that what we see can be as important as what we hear. As we are systematic in seeking information we will hear, we ought to be systematic in seeking information that we see. Our basic human faculties in social science field research are limited, so we should use them all to their fullest.[7]

Research Priorities

Research that can be completed at home before going into the field should have priority. All data that can be collected without asking for anyone else's time, which means without interviewing, should be undertaken with priority in the field. And all activities—reading and collecting documents, interviewing, and surveying—should take place simultaneously, as much as possible, once the order described here has been respected the first time through.

It should be clear, then, that considerable research precedes going into the field, that documentary research must continue in the field, and that in the field we are confined basically to reading, to listening, and to seeing. The problem lies in what we get to read, what we take the trouble to see, and to whom we get to listen. These concerns depend on how we present ourselves and how well we define exactly what we are doing. These most practical of matters will be our next principal concern.

Notes

1. A fourth means—employed by geographers, anthropologists, criminologists, and others—is taste. I have no experience with this method in social science and will not discuss it further.

2. See research beginning as early as 1945, as, for example, Muzafer Sherif and Hadley Cantril, "Psychology of Attitudes," *Psychological Review* 52 (November 1945):295–319 and 53 (January 1946):1–24.

3. I am using the term "survey" in preference to "questionnaire" because it is more embracing. "Questionnaire" implies a set of fixed questions eliciting coded or scaled responses. "Survey" suggests a variety of ways in which different problems, questions, or issues may be presented to a large number of people.

4. See especially Herbert H. Hyman et al., *Interviewing in Social Research* (Chicago: University of Chicago Press, 1954) pp. 83–137.

5. See the discussion in Hubert M. Blalock, Jr., *Social Statistics* (New York: McGraw-Hill Book Co., 1960) pp. 165–167.

6. Daniel Lerner and Morton Gordon, *Euratlantica: Changing Perspectives of the European Elites* (Cambridge, Mass.: MIT Studies in Comparative Politics, 1969). Robert Putnam did similar and more effective surveying later, reported in Robert D. Putnam, *Comparative Study of Political Elites* (Englewood Cliffs, N.J.: Prentice-Hall, 1976).

7. A useful source of ideas is Eugene J. Webb, Donald T. Campbell, Richard R. Schwartz, and Lee Sechrist, *Unobtrusive Measures* (Chicago: Rand McNally & Co., 1966).

3

The Conduct of Research

Once we have defined a subject of inquiry and have identified an object of study, certain problems present themselves in sequence. First, we must consider the precise methods for examining the object. If we have decided to use a survey, for example, we must prepare the instrument, pretest it, and prepare the requisite number of forms before going into the field. Appropriate and available literature should be read; accessible scholars and journalists familiar with the subject or the object should be visited.

All of these activities involve exploring the resources available where we are before we make the investment of going into the field. Field research must be thoroughly prepared so that the time in the field is spent profitably. Profitability, however, implies money, which is necessary if we are to go into the field. Unless we are independently wealthy, or unless we conduct the study near home, we need to raise funds for getting to the object of study, living there for a time, communicating with people, transporting ourselves to interviews, preparing forms, purchasing materials and documents, and so forth. The best-planned research can never see the light of day without an adequate supply of funds for such things.

Grantsmanship

Getting money often has very little to do with the quality of research, although few established social scientists would ever admit it. This fact should raise moral problems for those who give as well as for those who receive, but it does not change the practical issues of locating support for serious researchers. Until those who give show greater concern for the quality of the product of research, and until those who do research are uniformly more serious and honest in their undertakings, the necessity of playing the game known as "grantsmanship" will be difficult, if not impossible, to avoid.

It is hardest to get money the first time. That is, when you are unknown (and perhaps unpublished), it is especially difficult to interest someone in paying for the work you propose to undertake. The first necessity, therefore, is to find a patron. A patron can be anyone with an established reputation who inspires confidence on the part of those who have money to allocate. Entrusting funds for research does require some measure of confidence in the recipient. If you are unknown, the next best thing is to find someone who *is* known who will vouch for your project and the individual(s) planning to conduct it. It is up to you to find a patron.

With the support of the patron, you must then inventory those foundations, agencies, and individuals who support academic research in general and your area of research (subject *or* object) in particular. It is usually best to begin with governments. Federal and state agencies allocate substantial sums to research, and they are often looking for someone to carry out projects of interest.

Government agencies tend to pay for research in one of two ways: through contracts (which is the most popular way) or through outright grants. In general, contractual research is the product of—again—two possible methods. In the first, the agency issues a "request for proposal" (RFP). (This is especially true in the United States.) The RFP is normally sent to established scholars, consulting companies, research laboratories, and university departments. Often the RFP is "guided," which means very few people ever see it, and the agency hints strongly that a response to the RFP is likely to generate funds. Sometimes the RFP will even specify the sum available for support. An unknown researcher can get in on an RFP in basically one of two ways. He or she can either persuade the recipient to file the proposal and grant him or her supervision of the project, or the researcher can work on the project under the supervision of the RFP recipient. Obviously, the former is preferable; it is also more difficult to achieve because established scholars are understandably reluctant to risk their reputations on an unknown.

Apart from responding to an RFP, you might secure a contract from a government agency by submitting an unsolicited proposal in hopes that the agency will be interested in your specific area of concern. It is much more difficult to secure a contract this way. If you choose to pursue this route, however, you should consider how you might improve your chances of catching a bureaucrat's eye. At the least, you should try to know the name of the official likely to be responsible for receiving your proposal, and you should apply directly to that individual instead of to the whole agency. At the most, you should make contact with the most highly placed person in the agency whom you either know or can contact through someone else's acquaintance. You should enter into preliminary discussions to test for agency interest, and in this way, you may find someone in the hierarchy who will agree to guide your request personally. When someone in the agency takes a personal interest in your project, you stand a much better chance of securing funds than if you enter blindly hoping to catch someone's eye.

If a contract is issued, there are a number of concerns of which you should be aware. For one thing, a contract involves a specific agreement. The agency expects you to produce some specific thing. If, in the course of your research, you discover interesting questions that any good and responsible scholar might be inclined to pursue, the contract may not allow it. You might be obliged to defer, or even to cast aside completely, the study of this interesting path. The money has been given to find or study a particular problem, and the contract obliges you to stick to the specific task.

Because of the nature of contracts, scholars tend to seek vague terms and ambiguous promises. The scholar's independence and freedom is inversely related to the specificity of the contract. Moreover, the contract may put restrictions on the ownership of the materials, and the recipient may find it difficult, if not impossible, to publish results. Therefore, contracts need to be read carefully and negotiated.

The above restrictions—and many others—make contract research much less desirable than research done on outright grants. Contract research leans toward problem solving; grant research poses broader questions. Contract research is almost unscholarly by definition, for it involves research deliberately in service.[1] It is possible that the research interests will coincide precisely, but every deviation of interest between the contractor and the recipient is a challenge to intellectual independence.

As already indicated, there are two basic ways to secure money from governments: one is by contract, and the other is through outright grant. Sometimes grants are made through a general research agency, such as the national science foundations in the United States and West Germany. More often, however, grants are made through specific agencies concerned with specific problems. The greatest single source of funds for research in the United States, for example, is the Department of Defense, but it is erroneous to assume that the department itself controls strictly all research conducted with its money. On the contrary, much of the research paid for by the Pentagon yields results that are outside the apparently established interests of the agency. The key here lies more in the difference between contract and grant than between one agency and another. The terms of a grant should include the freedom of the researcher, with which no agency should—or normally will—interfere. For this reason, scholars should always prefer grants to contracts, and, indeed, some scholars will not work on contract under any circumstances.

There are also two ways to pursue a grant from a government agency. One, as described, involves a general inquiry. The second way can be more fruitful. The agency may sponsor a grant program whose terms provide for undertakings consistent with our research intentions. For example, the U.S. National Science Foundation may sponsor a program that provides research funds for doctoral dissertations. Whenever there is some specific program under which you can apply, it is preferable to file an application directly with the agency sponsoring that program. When an agency has established a granting program, it prefers to allocate research funds through such established procedures.

In all cases, whether we seek a contract or a grant, we need to make preliminary inquiries concerning agency interest and agency allocations. These inquiries are best made through personal contacts; they are admissible when writing to appropriate officials. If the agency has a particular format or wants particular supporting information, it is necessary to have complete details before filing. There are deadlines, usually early autumn, and it is important to meet them. Inquiries must begin, therefore, in spring or summer—some twelve months before support is needed. Finally, it is important to know whether more than one agency can receive the same application at the same time. In the Federal Republic of Germany, for example, only one government agency can consider a research proposal at a time. Application to more than one can damage severely the chances of securing support. When such restrictions on applications pertain, it is especially important to establish with which agency an application is likely to fare best.

While governments provide the greatest amount of research funds, they do not have a monopoly. Foundations and independent organizations have established research programs or are often willing to pay for certain kinds of research. The best place to begin an inquiry about such funding sources is among senior scholars. University bulletin boards also display information about grant programs, and most universities have development offices responsible for monitoring sources of potential funding. In addition, there are several volumes found in the reference section of most libraries that list foundations, their resources, their addresses, and the objectives of their support programs. It may be necessary to adjust the terms of a proposal somewhat in order to enhance the chances of eliciting interest in a given program or foundation, but the programs and foundations chosen should truly correspond to your interests. Nonetheless, if the terms of different programs are not precisely identical, it should be possible to adjust the scope of your project for the purpose of multiple applications.

The Research Proposal

Research proposals are essential for fund raising, but they also have a more general use. When formulating a project, we should always set to paper a detailed plan. First, we should write a one-page summary of the question we seek to answer and how we will try to answer it. This summary, sometimes called an "abstract" or a "précis," will guide all our subsequent preparation. Many students and scholars wait to prepare such a summary until after they have completed the research proposal or even, in some extreme cases, until after they have embarked on their research. The abstract loses much of its value if not prepared early, for it helps us to answer the questions we will most frequently hear from others: "What are you working on?" and "How are you doing it?" A succinct written statement of the subject and objects, with an indication of appropriate method, will be our most valued single document.

The research proposal itself should be short. Its purpose is to state the importance of the research, the status of the literature and the discipline in the given subject area, the questions to be raised, the method we will use, and the reasons we are especially worthy of support for this particular research. In other words, the proposal should be a clear description of our subject, our object, our method, our reasons, and our worthiness, and each of these areas should be blocked out separately.

The importance of the research refers to its significance, both for a general public and for our particular discipline. What proposal to fund cancer or heart research would not begin with dramatic statistics concerning fatalities from these and related diseases? If we want to study an ethnic group, we need to say at the outset how many people are members of this group and why learning about them will be useful for other peoples. Research on Canada surely must note the vast territory the country covers, the critical alliance that Canada shares with the United States, the valuable natural and human resources that help give it one of the world's highest standards of living.

If the research concerns a specific case, we must explain what it is a case *of*. Research may be intrinsically interesting, but it will only find an audience—or a sponsor—if it has potential for general lessons or can teach something new that will suggest understandings beyond the case itself. We must convince our readers—and ourselves—that this research is particularly worthy of support and attention and that it should be given preference over other efforts when scarce resources of time and money require selection among projects. Often this statement need only involve an articulation of how and why we chose the subject of research, since what made it important to us often will have a more general importance. Too often, students lose sight of the large questions posed by their research; this statement of importance becomes all the more useful for such cases.

In addition to explaining the importance of our research, we must also show that it has not been done before and that it will profit from previous work conducted in our own, or in a related, discipline. Hence, we need to demonstrate some familiarity, however modest, with relevant literature so that a reader can see where our project fits in the grand schemes of social science.

Having stipulated the questions we will ask, how we will ask them, why they are important, and the relevant accomplishments of our colleagues (and ourselves) to date, we must articulate an appropriate methodology so a reader will understand what exactly we intend to do with our time (and perhaps their money) in order to answer the questions or solve the problems we have chosen. This statement should include where the research will be conducted, whether we have secured cooperation from scholars or facilities there (or whether there is any cause to anticipate difficulty in doing so), and whether we have the requisite skills (language, statistics, interviewing, etc.). It is in this statement that we must demonstrate our own particular worthiness, convincing our readers—by citing prior accomplishment and preparation—that we are the right people to conduct this research.

Finally, our research proposal must include a budget. Many programs specify budget support, but more often we can expect to be asked, "How much money will you need?" It is always best to estimate on the high side, since if our estimates turn out low, it is almost always difficult to raise additional money (unless we indulge in the famous "cost overrun" of contractual research and development). Furthermore, proposals will rarely, if ever, be selected on the basis of sums involved. If a proposal generates interest but appears too expensive, we may be asked to propose another budget or another method to execute the research at less cost. But interest in the proposal is not likely to fall through because we ask for too much cash. In fact, the opposite often seems to be the case. If we ask for a sum of money that seems too little for the effective execution of the research, the proposal runs a risk of not being taken seriously. Agencies tend to think research ought to cost even more than it normally might. We should not forget to include, therefore, any overhead expenses we may be charged for working in a research center or institute. Finally, a research proposal will be considered in the same bureaucratic way whether much or little money is involved. First comes an examination of the merits of the idea and the interest or apparent value or importance of the research; then comes consideration of whether it can be afforded. (All this depends, of course, on whether the research proposal falls within the province of what the foundation or agency generally sponsors within its own charter.) Logically, a small sum of money ought to be more forthcoming than a large sum. This logic, however, does not normally apply in "grantsmanship."

Researchers are often asked when making a proposal, "What is the thesis?" or "What do you expect to show or find out?" These questions ask us to have some sense of the research results before we have actually done the research. Needless to say, it is almost impossible to know the results beforehand. We may entertain a number of theories or hypotheses, but it is generally contrary to our assumptions about free inquiry to have the answers before we begin. Nevertheless, there is an apparent reluctance on the part of granters of funds to accept this ignorance.

Let me suggest here one possible solution to this problem that may seem facetious but should be considered seriously. As I said earlier, the first grant is always the hardest. There is something of a cumulative effect after the first grant. When an agency recognizes that others have thought us worthy of support before, it is easier to instill confidence than when our slates are blank. For this reason, we are hard-pressed the first time around. Since it is much easier to explain what a particular research project can discover after it has been done than before (and also easier to know what it will cost after it has been done and money has been spent), it is easier to seek funds for research already completed. The funds allocated can then go into a new project or a more advanced phase of the present one. If we are prepared to withhold our results until the next project or final completion of the present work (thus staying one project ahead in the use of funds), we will be able to budget precisely and propose subject, object, hypothesis, and thesis with little difficulty.

Let's call this idea the "one-project-ahead" or "one-grant-ahead" method. If the new funds pay for the last project—that is, if the monies we use for a new project are based on an old one—we are more likely to please those who pay and our own results may be of better quality. Since precise proposals are better than vague ones, we should not discount the potential value of such an approach to grantsmanship. This approach raises moral issues, but the practice is much more common than might be supposed, and its practitioners do not consider themselves immoral. We should always remember, however, that poor-quality research may make it difficult to secure subsequent support.

Setting Up Shop

Once we have the money and can go into the field there are a number of immediate problems that must be solved. The greatest of these is almost always finding living accommodations. An official affiliation with the use of an office is invaluable, for it may provide an official address, the use of telephone, and possibly other services. In many cities there are institutes that provide space for visiting researchers, and every attempt should be made to use that space. Access can often be gained directly by writing in advance or even by arriving at the door. However, chances of securing space to work and use facilities improve substantially when (1) the foundation or agency providing financial support either provides space itself or makes a request at an institute in our behalf, and (2) some personal contact within the institute in question can provide help. However it is secured, office space reduces enormously the burden of living accommodations.

If there is no office space, then the housing problem takes on special dimensions. Single researchers might be able to take a room in someone's home; for couples or families such an arrangement is more difficult. If we intend to do any interviewing, a telephone becomes a necessity. In Europe, a telephone may not be in a given apartment, and the cost and wait for installation is forbidding. Since one room is likely to become a constant work space, at least two rooms will be needed. In an urban setting an automobile may be hard to operate or afford; if research is to be concentrated at certain libraries, institutions, or agencies or in certain neighborhoods, it will be important to live near these places or at least near good public transportation. These prerequisites can drive up the cost of housing as well as increase the difficulty in finding something. Time spent looking for accommodations is time lost from research. On the other hand, long daily travel or inadequate work space can present a constant drain on resources as well.

To meet these needs we should be prepared, yet again, to exploit contacts. Do we know anyone living in the place where we are going? Might they know of a suitable or sufficient accommodation? Is there a university with a housing office that might help? It is hard to accept housing before arrival, though something temporary is always needed.

The search for housing can vary widely from city to city and country to country. In London, for example, the *Evening Standard* newspaper, which appears in the early afternoon, has many pages of advertisements for housing. Unfortunately, many of the listings lead back to a few agencies that seek fees, and the many telephone calls necessary to learn this advertising device can prove frustrating and expensive. The *London Times*, whose listings are far more brief (and whose daily edition costs twice as much), often proves more reliable and useful. In addition there are numerous agencies, both within the immediate areas where we might want accommodation and in the Center for the Greater London area, but since they all work (except the "estate agents") on commission from those who seek a place to live, they seek to convince clients to take more expensive accommodations.

Often embassies and consulates provide housing lists. In Florence, for example, the British consulate maintains an informal list on which Americans (who find no like service in the bigger American consulate down the road) frequently rely. It also can help to place an advertisement in the local newspaper, stating who you are (e.g., "American research student . . .") and what kind of accommodation you seek. Many people reluctant to advertise their housing may respond to the reversed roles. I can attest personally to the efficacy of this method—much to my own surprise—in Italy.

Living arrangements, though they may seem trivial, constitute one of the most serious problems of field research. They cause considerable anxiety and lost time. As much as possible should be done before arriving in a new place, but you should also be resigned to the likelihood of difficulty once you do arrive.

The Researcher's Affiliation

Once housing is found it is possible to set out on the task of research itself. But there remains yet another preliminary problem. We must decide how we will present ourselves—that is, what or whom we represent and with whom or what we are associated. There is no simple answer. Suppose we come from a university, have a grant from a foundation, and have office space in an institute. Here we have at least three different affiliations. And what are we doing? "Research" is rarely a satisfactory identification for people being questioned. In general, we had better be writing a dissertation or a book. The questions "Why are you doing this?" and "Whom are you doing this for?" will be asked repeatedly. We had better be armed with good answers.

This problem of identity can be extremely complicated. Suppose, for instance, we have a grant to study political conflicts over airports from the airport authority. The grant is without qualifications, and we are pursuing independent and free research under the auspices of a university. But we need to ask questions of local people in conflict with the airport authority. If we answer one of the above questions with, "The research is paid for by the airport authority," we can rest assured we will receive no worthwhile answers from hostile and suspicious local citizens. For the local citizens, then, we are doing university research. But we also need to raise questions with the airport authority's bureaucracy, which is suspicious of universities. There we must give the answer we could never have contemplated giving to the local citizens. We are obliged to divide our multiple identity.

In another example, suppose we do research sponsored by the Department of Labor concerning local manpower programs. To local groups, people who work for the government are not to be trusted; to local government agencies, independent researchers are not worthy of precious time to answer questions. So we are independent for the locals and we work for the government as far as the agencies are concerned. Our entire identity, if revealed, could destroy our research, not because we do necessarily work for anyone or out of anyone's interest, but because people answering questions normally doubt the concept of independent or free inquiry and because the research sponsor may indeed seek to influence our research. If we study German-Israeli relations with a German grant, the Israelis are inevitably suspicious. If we study automobile workers with a grant from FIAT, the workers must certainly be suspicious. So we must identify with some independent institution.

Multiple identities often can be exploited valuably, even though the use of them may raise moral questions. Are we less than honest if we are less than candid for the sake of data collection? How much must we tell, given that we expect others to tell us everything? And if we tell less than everything, what happens if we are found out?

Above all, we must be consistent. That is, even if we don't tell all, we must never tell something other than the truth. We must never claim to work for the government if we do not; we must never claim to be enrolled in a university if we are not. The sources of money can complicate enormously our research tasks, no matter how honestly we pursue our research. Consequently, we must be especially careful. If we work for a newspaper, it is foolish and immoral to pretend we do not. Once found out, we can never proceed again. It is normally best to be independent and to be affiliated with a nonaligned or impartial institute or university. Unfortunately, this ideal is rarely achieved when money is needed. Not only must we resist any attempts to be influenced by those who pay us; we must resist permitting the sources of money from interfering in any way with the pursuit of honest research.

We should note that it is almost always necessary to carry some form of identification. This identification should be fancy enough to impress and simple enough not to confuse. In general, the solution is the personal calling card. Before setting out to see people, you should have cards printed with your name, address, and phone number (if you know them in advance), and your most neutral official affiliation. Prestigious affiliations always have a certain value, but we should be constantly aware that prestige in the field relates more to neutrality than to power; better to identify—on a card that may be circulated—with a university than with a government or agency.

Furthermore, whatever titles you have should be displayed. Asking people to cooperate with research involves a demand on their time for which you offer meager compensation at best. Unless people just like to be helpful or just like to talk—which happens less often than might be desirable—you are obliged to convince them that you deserve their help. The best, and most honest, way to convince people to help is by convincing them of a serious purpose. Serious purposes are associated with serious people and serious institutions. If you appear important—because you have degrees or titles or come from a notable institution—you are more likely to elicit cooperation than if you appear to be just another student, bent on interfering with people's time and lives. We may doubt the justice in a world of such bias, but we would be foolhardy to doubt the truth of it or to fail to draw appropriate conclusions in order to conduct ourselves.

The calling card should not necessarily tell all, but it should tell that which can be told to everyone. A fair supply should always be at hand, and we should not hesitiate to use them. In general, however, one hundred cards are a lot of cards. They will last at least a year in most research.

In addition to carrying calling cards to identify us, it is also helpful to carry letters of reference or introduction. If we know someone who knows someone else that we want to see, we should carry a letter of introduction. The institutions with which we are affiliated should provide general letters asking for cooperation on our behalf from other institutions, libraries, individuals, etc. We should head into the field armed with these letters, and if someone can write ahead personally on our behalf, that opportunity should be seized.

Launching the Inquiry

Research should begin always by identifying the local resources: Where are the archives? Where are documents kept? What is kept in which libraries? We should make ourselves known to curators and librarians and arrange visiting and (if possible) borrowing privileges.

If there is a local newspaper, we should read it. We will learn, at the very least, the local issues of the day, which will make our contact with people easier because we will be familiar with what is important to them. At the most, we will find stories about the subject of our study. We also will learn the names and roles of key actors.

We should then contact the local nonpartisan experts on our subject. University people and journalists tend to be the two principal resources. Then we can hope to frame issues better by acquiring a better understanding and feel for local perceptions and a sense of who is perceived as knowledgeable and important. In this way we can begin to compile a systematic list of the people we want to see and what, more precisely, we should ask them.

In setting out to visit archives, libraries, and local specialists, it is often best to announce ourselves in writing first. The pattern (which should be repeated when seeking interviews in the field) should involve writing a short letter identifying ourselves and our project, asking for an appointment, and explaining precisely what we intend to do at a meeting if it is granted. We should propose a time and date, invite a reply, and promise to telephone for confirmation within some specified time if no written reply has been received.

A follow-up telephone call, if necessary, should not descend into an interview. To this end, it is often best to ask on the phone for a secretary or someone who keeps a person's calendar. If the party we want to see gets on the other end of the phone, he or she is likely to launch a series of questions obliging us, in effect, to present our own questions then and there. Telephone exchanges have many disadvantages, the greatest of which is the most obvious: We cannot establish eye contact, so we cannot judge effectively when a question might lead somewhere else and when something is, at least for the moment, better left alone. Whenever possible, telephone interviews are to be avoided. The best way to avoid them, again, is never to get on the phone with the party in the first place. If it is unavoidable, we should state our business as succinctly as possible with an eye to arranging a convenient meeting.

The practice of writing letters is especially valuable because it assures that the party we intend to see will have something in front of them with which to associate our voice on the phone or, later, our presence in the room. It sets a formal, businesslike, and serious tone to the task. If the letter can be sent on some kind of official letterhead, so much the better. In any event, formality suggests respect for the other parties. When people feel respected, they cooperate and help. We should always make every effort, therefore, to generate a feeling of respect.

For many research projects, we can begin almost immediately to contact some sources of information; other cases may require a slower approach. If the research concentrates on a bureaucratic or government elite, we can move ahead formally and officially without a major concern for ingratiating ourselves. If, on the other hand, we are studying local activists, workers, trade unions, or political parties—or for that matter any group of people out of power and struggling for it—the approach must be different. There is a certain, often justified, paranoia among such groups. They often have been infiltrated or subverted. Their self-conscious challenge to established authority makes them especially suspicious of our purpose and method. They may have a clear but unspoken hierarchy that we are expected to observe and respect. We walk into such settings largely ignorant, and a few early mistakes—which offend people or cast doubt on our seriousness or honesty or generate a lack of trust and confidence—can destroy our entire research effort.

In settings where we are studying local groups out of power, we must present ourselves discreetly and somewhat less formally. We must inquire quietly how things are arranged and organized and who is recognized as the local leadership. We might have to visit the bars or cafés, the local church on Sunday, and so forth. The accounts of such research are numerous, ranging from *Street Corner Society*[2] and *Tally's Corner*[3] to Edgar Morin's *The Red and the White*.[4] We should familiarize ourselves with this literature and with the experiences of others in pursuing this kind of delicate research before we set out ourselves.

Since we must establish trust, we usually need to allow a great deal more time for local community research than for elite study. The need for more time has been demonstrated amply by Laurence Wylie in *Village in the Vaucluse* and *Chanzeaux*.[5] We need to find a place to live, and we also need to build trust and a network of contacts. A general rule of thumb is that setting up shop for good community field research can be expected to take three or four months. Only then will we have established ourselves in the community such that people will be open, lead us to other people, and so forth. Since we are normally obliged to indicate how long a research project will take before we launch it, these factors must be taken into consideration.

As I have emphasized before, the choice of research object is closely tied to the choice of subject. Similarly, we should be conscious of the choice of site. Whether we work in a big city, a small neighborhood, or a small town depends, of course, on the questions we want answered. But we should remain conscious here that the choice of site affects in major ways the conduct of research and the time needed. Moreover, it affects when we begin our research or move to a particular site. It may be necessary to arrive before the end of a term of parliament when all the legislators return to their constituencies or before the end of the university term when students and faculty scatter to their homes; or it may be important to know when landlords and landladies tend to holiday, lest we arrive without hope of finding a place to live for a while. Elite research in Europe during the Christmas holidays is a futile undertaking, just as it would be in Washington in August. These local conditions are also part of the information we need to launch research, to structure our time, and to calculate our timing.

Getting Interviews

As in contacting resource people shortly after our arrival, we should also arrange interviews more directly related to data collection through formal approaches. The formal and official request for the allocation of time is universally flattering. Flattery can, in research, get us everywhere, so we should write a letter and follow it with a telephone call. Often, of course, this procedure is not possible, and in some communities it is not necessary. In Washington, D.C., for example, much can be arranged directly by telephone because the American capital prides itself on a daytime, efficient informality. Such informal approaches in Paris would be—in far too many cases—disastrous. We can never go wrong being formal. Informality involves risk. In general, especially at the beginning, it is best to follow these formal procedures.

Getting interviews can often be facilitated through third parties, which is one reason why we should begin with those people we think most likely to be sympathetic to our enterprise. Whenever a third party offers to arrange an interview, it is usually worthwhile to accept the offer. Accepting the help makes the helper feel as though he or she is contributing, and it helps make the person to be interviewed feel somewhat responsible both to the interviewer and to the intervening third party. Such dual obligation can and often should be exploited.

Some networks may seem impenetrable. Potential respondents communicate with each other and seem to conspire not to see us. Alternatively, each time we arrive at an office we are greeted with a reference to the person we just left. There is no solution to the inconvenience of communications among respondents, but there are ways in which we can penetrate a network. One particularly valuable approach is to exploit the "young boys' network." Somewhere within the orbit of the parties concerned we may have an acquaintance or two. They may have been classmates in high school or college or graduate school. They may be former students, teachers, cousins, or even friends of friends. If we can locate them anywhere in an appropriate bureaucracy, we may discover they can reach into the network of respondents for us.

We may be inclined to neglect these contacts because they are not situated in the upper echelons of the bureaucracy. They are not, themselves, the elites we seek. However, it is important to remember that the directors of agencies, like the generals of armies, usually are not familiar with day-to-day operations. Agencies are run by the colonels, not the generals, and the colonels often can prove to be the most valuable sources of information. The "old boys' network" may be beyond our reach, but it may also be populated by generals. The young boys' network, closer to our own generation, may contain the lieutenants and colonels.

Some people may not want to give an interview but would prefer to be credited with being too busy rather than unwilling. We must decide in such cases how important such a person really is for us. If important enough, there are time-honored journalistic methods for getting to see someone. We can wait religiously at the office or at the home. We can offer to ride along *en route* somewhere, carry a suitcase, or open a door. We can have others write letters or place telephone calls on our behalf. We can simply telephone every day. Whatever we do, we must be fair. Hence, before applying pressure tactics we must have offered to meet at any time, in any reasonably accessible place. If we have been this accommodating, we can then more vigorously seek an audience.

Businessmen, lawyers, and doctors will occasionally inform us of the unique cash value of their time. They will be happy to see us, they may say, if we are prepared to pay the one hundred dollars per hour (or whatever the sum) to which they are accustomed. Each researcher must decide whether an audience with a particular individual is worth such an investment, for it may prove, on very rare occasion, worth taking up such a challenge. In general, however, it should be remembered that no single person, like no single document, is likely to be worth the expense.

Another point to consider is that we may be granted an appointment for only a very brief interval. Rarely do such interviews terminate when scheduled, however, so we should accept such appointments rather than think the time allowed to be too short and consequently not go at all.

It is also possible that we will be asked to submit our questions in writing before the interview. We should never hesitate to comply, remembering that if we are given an audience we will probably have the opportunity to probe. By "probing" (which will be discussed later) I mean the exploration of certain answers to gain clarification or further information. Probing is always necessary in open-ended interviews and is frequently necessary in closed interviews.

We may resent the suggestion that respondents are vulnerable to attractive members of the opposite sex. On the other hand, female interviewers often do have difficulty getting respondents to take them seriously, and men may be subject to the problem of sex bias as well. In instances where a man or woman has difficulty getting an appointment and senses a sex bias, he or she should find someone of the opposite sex to telephone or accompany him or her to the interview. This person should be identified as a research partner. For interviewing executives, there is nothing better than the presence of an attractive person of the opposite sex. For interviewing government officials and others in male-dominated circles, attractive young women may do better if accompanied by serious-looking young men. The researcher can conduct the inquiry and can indeed do all the talking. It is the presence of the other person that makes the difference.

Finally, we should recognize that many people will answer written requests despite a refusal to meet with us. Although the face-to-face interview is preferable, the value of written answers should not be discounted. If we are able to put precisely both our informational and attitudinal requests, we have every reason to expect useful replies. When someone has refused to see us due to time constraints, we should write asking if written questions would be acceptable. Upon the granting of our request, the questions should then be sent as quickly as possible.

The Place of the Interview

It is sometimes possible to choose where the interview will be held. Usually this choice will be between a respondent's home or office. There are advantages and disadvantages to both, but in general, if it is possible to see someone at home, the likelihood of a more forthright exchange is improved. Away from the office a respondent is inclined to feel removed from others who might overhear. Even though documents and reference materials may all be at the office (which may create a handicap), a person interviewed at home may prove willing to assemble pertinent documents in the office later on. For these reasons, despite the risk of being deprived access to some documents, the home should normally be preferred whenever choice is available.

Many interviews will probably be conducted over meals, especially lunch and occasionally dinner. When we are invited, we should try to accept, but we should remember at least two points. (1) It is very difficult to take notes and out of the question to operate a tape recorder during a meal. Although food and drink may lead a respondent to be especially lucid, it is best, whenever possible, to arrange for the meeting to continue after eating. This way, important ground can be repeated, and notes can be taken. If the interview cannot be continued after the meal, however, the interviewer is faced with being wholly dependent on memory, which is likely to be impaired by food and drink. (2) If the interview takes place at a restaurant, the respondent—who has usually extended the invitation—will normally propose to pay the bill. Purists will feel that to permit such payment may create a measure of indebtedness; the respondent may expect us to tell our story casting him or her in a favorable light. We must each make our own judgment on this question. I think that when respondents perceive us in their debt, they often are even more forthcoming; it is up to us to overcome the bourgeois response that associates financial outlay with moral indebtedness. A single meal is not a vicuna coat; if we distort the story, we are more culpable as poor social scientists than as takers of bribes. One caveat, however: If we are working on contract, these matters are more delicate than if we are wholly independent. And if we are on expense accounts, we should be prepared both to extend the invitations and to pick up the bill.

The Interview Itself

Once the interview is arranged, several rules should be followed: (1) be on time; (2) do not be early; (3) dress as if you are going to be interviewed for a good office job; and (4) follow all the standard operating procedures for going after something you want. That is, although you conduct the interview, you must *behave* as if you were being interviewed in the hope of, say, securing a job. After all, you are asking for something and normally not offering much in return. As interviewers we are generally guests in other people's offices or homes. So we sit when invited, and we terminate the interview and leave if asked. Smoking is a bad idea. We should not doodle during a boring discourse, or stare out windows, or wander around distractedly, even when accompanying someone else who may be asking the questions. All attention must be focused on the respondent and, in general, we should follow the lead of our respondent. Every move must be calculated as a reflection of respect for the other party. And even if we do not really feel any particular respect, we should recognize that we seek something, and, however painful it may be, we should humble ourselves accordingly. Rebellion and the conduct of research are not especially compatible, even though the questions we ask and the manner in which we deal with the results might be very rebellious indeed.

The Language of the Interview

With regard to the conduct of interviews, one point should be emphasized concerning foreign languages. We must appreciate that weakness can be turned to advantage. Whereas it is best for the respondent to speak clearly in his or her native language, that may not always be best for us. We are always inclined, of course, to attempt the language of the respondent. But if we are invited to proceed in our own language, we ought to recognize the advantages: (1) we will obviously understand more; (2) we will be able to ask our questions more precisely; and (3) we will control more thoroughly the course of the interview. A respondent can always explain or clarify in native tongue an obscure or difficult-to-express point. Furthermore, we will not need to translate the data later. Offers to speak in our native language may come from the Italians, for example; they are less likely to come from the French, and when they do they may also yield disdainful answers thereafter. In some instances, of course, delicate subjects will be discussed more openly with someone who seems a "member of the family" (speaks the native language). Germans do not like to explain antisemitism to outsiders (i.e., non–German speakers). In general, nevertheless, speaking in the language most comfortable for us is beneficial. We should recognize, too, that some languages may be neutral or preferable for the discussion of sensitive subjects, whereupon neither the interviewer nor the respondent will speak in native tongue. Finally, if we profess weakness in a language, we can be forgiven asking deceptively simple questions that are often valuable but resented when language comprehension is assumed or apparent. Thus, any weakness we have with a language should be exploited to invite repetition, clarification, and simplicity where otherwise points may have been deliberately obfuscating.

Getting and Exchanging Information

As I said earlier, we offer very little in exchange for the information and cooperation we ask. A respondent might imagine being recorded for posterity or might hope to gain some advantage over opponents. A respondent might find us more worthy than a journalist and hope we will retell a story to set straight a previously distorted record. For these reasons we should begin interviews by restating the purpose of our research and by reassuring the respondent of his or her singular importance and knowledge. When a respondent is self-deprecating (seriously or facetiously), we should indicate how pleased we are with the opportunity to interview him or her, perhaps offering specific examples of the respondent's appropriate expertise. On the other hand, a respondent may have no need or desire to inform despite flattery. Although granting an appointment, a respondent may not be prepared to say much. We have only one thing available to pry loose information, and that is information itself.

A respondent is always interested in knowing what other people have been saying and is always keen to pry loose information that might have come to us in confidence. Because the confidentiality of our work and its integrity are almost all we have, we must protect with extreme caution any assault on it. We should not quote and attribute information from one interview in another. If asked, "What did X say?" we must indicate that we are not at liberty to respond. Unfortunately that answer is precisely the answer we can then anticipate from our respondent to our questions.

To get around this problem, we should be prepared to reveal information, though always without attribution. We can say, "We have heard from some people . . ." without jeopardizing confidentiality. In general we should prefer not to trade information this way, but we must be prepared to do so. It should be done sparingly and only when necessary. It also must be done cautiously so that the respondent does not fear that we might do the same with his or her testimony. But information is all we have to trade and we must be prepared to trade it.

Comparative research has particular advantages in solving this problem. Information collected in another city or another country is far less sensitive than information collected in the same neighborhood or in the same parliament or within the same union or club. But we should recognize that such information piques curiosity no less. Thus, we should exploit, though again with a sparing tongue, the fact that we may be familiar with a similar case about which a respondent may be curious but know nothing at all. Furthermore, the less the respondent knows in advance, the less need be told to seem like making a trade.

The reverse of the last point should be emphasized. The less we know the less we can hope to learn. Later interviews will be more productive than earlier ones, which means that, in general, we should save the most knowledgeable people for last or arrange to see them at the beginning—when they may save us considerable time—and again at the end, when we have more to discuss. Respondents will detect the depth and breadth of our knowledge just as we will detect our respondents' familiarity with particular subjects when the inevitable trading of information develops. It is better to trade the information that is most remote to the respondent for that with which he or she is most familiar. Apparent openness on our part normally can bring such an exchange about. However, we must always remember that this rule is most useful to comparative research where our access to remote yet interesting information is greatest.

Let us consider for a moment the problem of "probing," especially in the context of closed interviews or when written questions have been submitted in advance. Let us imagine the following exchange. Written question: "Do you approve of General de Gaulle's nuclear policy?" Spoken answer: "I have always believed France must be strong and must use whatever means available to deter aggressors." We might interpret this answer affirmatively inasmuch as General de Gaulle's policy involves French strength, or we might interpret it negatively inasmuch as the program is deliberately limited in scale and scope. We do not repeat the question. Rather, we might go on to say, "General de Gaulle's nuclear policy involves cutting back the overall defense budget. Do you oppose defense cuts, and would you question the nuclear policy if it contributed directly to such cuts?" This question was not on our submitted list, but an answer will probably be offered. It is possible that the respondent will challenge our probe on the grounds that it is a different question; therefore, we should always be prepared to explain honestly and directly the meaning and purpose of our probe.

Even in a closed interview such probing may be necessary. For example, we ask, "How many people do you support in your household?" Answer: "Well, there is my wife, two daughters, my mother-in-law every evening, and my son's college roommate every weekend." We have to do some mental arithmetic, and we do not have an answer we can record. Does the mother-in-law live elsewhere and dine with our respondent every evening? Or perhaps he is being facetious and complaining about his wife's long-distance telephone calls. Is the son at home? Does the roommate visit every weekend all year? When the answer we are given is unclear or impossible to code, we must be prepared to ask further questions that are not necessarily on our form in order to secure the information we seek. We might ask the respondent in this instance, "You support five people including yourself, then?" The respondent will then sort out an answer.

We should always be cautious when probing. The manner in which a question is posed may influence the answer. For example, our French respondent might say "yes" if we ask, "General de Gaulle is really a great man, don't you think so?" A less leading question might have produced a more subtle answer. Or let us suppose that we are asking whether respondents perceive a "special relationship" between Canada and the United States. If we ask about the "special relationship" directly, they may discuss relations between the two countries as "special." If we never refer to the relations as "special," however, perhaps the respondents will not either. If they do not, it may indicate that relations are not perceived this way; the phrasing of our question may have precluded the possibility of discovering whether our very terms helped create answers.[6]

As researchers we must be self-conscious about avoiding advocacy. Often we will find ourselves with people who are making statements with which we strongly disagree. We may want to take issue with them. We must always remember the purpose of our business. We came to inquire and to find out, not to advocate. However painful it may seem at the time—or, for that matter, even in retrospect—we must reserve the advocacy for the presentation of our results when the data collection is complete. The sometimes fine distinction between prodding and advocating must be respected.

Keeping a Record of the Interview

An important decision concerns how we will keep a record of the interview. One possible way is to bring someone along who will take notes; another is to work as a team with someone else; a third way is to take notes ourselves; a fourth method involves using a tape recorder; and a fifth method is to write out everything from memory after the interview. Let us consider these possibilities in order.

The Silent Partner. It is generally not a good idea to bring along a notetaker. The silent, recording presence in the room, however self-consciously unobtrusive, is likely to constrain responses even more than the tape recorder, which we will discuss in a moment. The notetaker is like an audience, and however trusted the person may be, the respondent is unlikely to feel capable of speaking confidentially. There are exceptions, of course. But generally other methods for keeping records are preferable.

Interviewing as a Team. Team interviewing is quite different from having someone along as notetaker, as we will see in a moment. Team interviewing has the special advantage of allowing one person to take notes while the other concentrates on a line of questioning. But team interviewing can be difficult and usually requires more preparation than an interview conducted alone. More preparation is needed because we must coordinate carefully with our partner. On the one hand, we do not want to let a line of questioning fall unpursued, yet we must be wary not to interfere with the technique and style of our partner (who may inquire more or less directly, more or less quickly, than we would). On the other hand, we want to avoid the pregnant pauses when we anticipate incorrectly what our partners may do next. Lines of questioning must be agreed upon in advance, and the interview should have a leader. Moreover, the leader should arrange the interview, for the respondent will assume that the same party who made the arrangements will also conduct the interview (respondents always will consider a professor the leader when accompanied by an assistant, however).

Partners should be aware of each other's technique and style and should avoid interfering as much as possible. Many of these problems are subtle. Team interviewing can benefit from the presence of two minds and two pens, but it can also suffer from a lack of coordination. This method works especially well when there are linguistic problems requiring extra concentration but can be especially awkward when crossed signals lead to saying or asking the wrong things. Above all, we must not correct our partner or indicate any disagreement; nor should we offer an answer to our partner's question. There may be a reason of which we are unaware for asking a particular question in a particular way, and in any case we must be what the name implies—a team. Team interviewing, therefore, may seem a relief to the novice, but it is usually most effective when done by a skilled pair. The inexperienced researcher is most often better off alone.

Notetaking. Whether you take notes yourself or in coordination with a partner, you must come prepared. Before setting out for an interview you should always check for plenty of paper and pens with ink that will not run out. The paper should be attached in a notebook of manageable size that can rest comfortably on your lap during the course of the interview; you cannot expect to have a writing surface available, and you should never presume to set yourself up on someone's desk or table. In fact, notes should be taken as inconspicuously as possible, which means it is best to take them in a small notebook on your lap or in your hands, away from open view.

The page onto which you will record the notes should be prepared in advance. We are not acrobats, but social scientists; we cannot, therefore, plan to juggle papers while posing questions and taking notes. We must remember that there are two sets of notes at an interview: the notes we are taking and the notes that are guiding our questions. Since many interviews on the same subject will need to be completed before a researcher can rely on memory to conduct an interview, where shall we keep the notes we are using? If possible, they should be written on the same page as the notes we are taking. I like to carve out a corner where I list my questions in short form, leaving the rest of the page to record answers. In this way I have nothing to juggle.

Many researchers feel insecure without a list of fully written questions. Writing out questions can be helpful, and no interview can be prepared without serious reflection on what the questions will be about and what purpose must be accomplished. However, writing out questions in full normally precludes taking notes on the same page. The size of the sheet containing the questions should be approximately the same size as that on which the answers will be recorded. The questions should be kept within easy view, organized in front of us so that we can take notes without shuffling papers to find the questions or to find blank paper.

It is very important not to pursue an interview by burying our heads in our questions or notes. We must concentrate on what we are being told if we hope to ask coherent and logical questions. Therefore, when we take our notes, we must plan to take *only* notes—not long statements verbatim. Our priorities must lie with the relationship we can establish and maintain with our respondent. Furthermore, if our respondent indicates at some point that something about to be said is strictly confidential or off the record, it is important that we give some physical sign acknowledging this wish. If we are taking notes, the best way is to set down pens conspicuously, even fold hands, so that it is clear we are listening and not writing. After the confidential statement is complete, during some other discussion, we can then record quickly the main points not recorded earlier. Confidential remarks cannot be used with attribution, but in other ways or for other purposes they may well be remarks we want to remember.

We should recognize that taking notes and paying attention to what is being said while thinking of the next question involve mental acrobatics no less challenging than the shuffling of papers. And just as we can reduce the paper problem by preparing these materials thoughtfully before arriving at the interview, we can also make some preparations for the mental problems.

If we plan to refer to our notes only rarely in order to concentrate on the respondent, we must make a special effort to know the content of our notes, committing the better part of our questions to memory. Before setting out for certain kinds of elite interviews, we should also make a routine of checking *Who's Who*, or some appropriate equivalent, so that we are fully familiar with a respondent's background. Something is liable to come up during an interview that relates to a respondent's past, and it is much better to be fully acquainted with that past so we are not obliged to make superficial historical inquiry. We should also be familiar with public statements made by the subject and should be familiar with whatever the respondent has written. Government officials may publish under a pseudonym; we should try to locate and read any such writings. It is better to commit these things to memory than to rely on notes during an interview, and the more we can cite the individual's own background the better, for it flatters the respondent at the same time that it advances the discussion beyond public knowledge that otherwise would be repeated.

Using a Tape Recorder. The tape recorder is a technological device designed to meet many problems. In theory it should solve all problems of notetaking at interviews. Unfortunately, it is not the panacea it may seem, though in some instances it can be invaluable. Let us consider first when it might be used, and then what some of its advantages and disadvantages are.

Again, in theory, the tape recorder might be used at any interview. It is often helpful to ask over the telephone when completing the final arrangements for an interview whether it will be possible to bring a tape recorder. Such warning is sometimes preferable to merely arriving with tape recorder in hand, but the respondent who asks that a tape recorder not be used might have felt differently had we arrived ready to go. It is difficult to judge which strategy to adopt; my own experience suggests that there may be a small advantage in arriving with the tape recorder in hand. It is impossible to tape, of course, if the respondent—for whatever reason—prefers not to have the tape recorder present. In general, officials in England and in Italy will reject the use of a tape recorder on the grounds of confidentiality; in France there is in contrast a certain enthusiasm sometimes expressed, as if to suggest that the tape recorder is proof of a serious purpose and that remarks will be reported accurately and for posterity. In the United States there is relative indifference.

When the tape recorder is allowed (and even with it in hand we must ask whether we can use it before setting it up), we must take a number of mechanical precautions. First, we must be sure the batteries are fresh. We should also have enough clear tape, which usually requires overestimating the probable duration of the interview. The equipment must be prepared so that we need only plug in the microphone, press the record button, and begin. Whatever tape recorder we have, we should be sure that (1) it registers voice to be sure it is recording, and (2) it shows clearly that the tape is turning. During the course of the interview we should be sure to shut off the tape recorder when told something confidential, and we must remember that restarting usually requires holding down the record button again. Finally, in the category of mechanical concerns, we should know how long our tape will run and remember to turn it over or change it (for this reason, among others, we should be sure to wear a watch to an interview). These points may appear obvious or trivial, but on the first few tries, some or all of these errors are likely. The major portion of an interview can be lost by forgetting to bring enough tape or forgetting to turn over or change the tape. Finally, we need to mark the tape after it has been used so that we do not accidentally erase an interview.

The tape recorder is especially helpful when we are dealing in foreign languages. In fact, foreign language use is often an ideal excuse for securing consent ("Forgive me, but since my French is not that good . . ."). It is also helpful for recording material that can be quoted directly without paraphrase, since it helps us to concentrate more on the line of questions than on taking notes. Finally, a tape recorder may encourage people (as is often the case in France) to speak out.

There are many disadvantages as well. The tape recorder can inhibit a respondent (even when the respondent may claim otherwise), so for this reason the tape recorder we use should be small and unobtrusive. We should put the microphone midway between ourselves and the respondent (and leave it there, not keep emphasizing its presence by moving it about or making adjustments), and we should let the cord run so that the recorder itself is more or less out of the respondent's view. Locating the recorder this way cuts down on the motor's background noise feeding through the microphone as well.

We should also remember that tape recorders tend to lull us into a technological dependence with two major drawbacks: (1) if for some reason the recording fails or the quality of the tape is poor, we may have no notes or material from the interview, and (2) we cannot digest the many, many hours of tape recording that we will accumulate in the course of a project. For these reasons we cannot permit the tape recorder to substitute completely for notetaking. Not only do we need a few notes to jog our memories in case of mechanical failure, but also, when something of particular interest is said, we should record in our notes the number on the tape counter so that we can find the important segment of tape later on without having to listen to the whole tape.

It is impossible to know in any given case whether it would be better to tape or not to tape. We must make personal judgments concerning the respondents. We always risk inhibition, but we always stand to gain a documentary record. In addition to taking into account the general national and cultural tendencies suggested above, the researcher must judge each case independently.

Writing Notes After the Interview. The final method we have suggested for recording an interview is to write out everything after the interview is over. This method relies, of course, on superior memory. Even the best of us will probably need a few notes to remember everything. Summarizing our notes should be standard practice after all interviews, however, regardless of how we take notes during the interviews.

Concluding the Interview

Whatever method we have chosen for keeping a record of our interview, there are some standard procedures that might be followed as the interview comes to a conclusion. First we should always clarify whether we can quote our respondent. We should also ask whether it will be possible to return if the research seems to require a subsequent visit. (Each interview should be conducted, however, on the assumption that we will never see a given person again, unless we have already arranged a series of meetings.) If a series of meetings is planned, we may set aside areas of inquiry, but if there is no such prior agreement we cannot assume later access; for this reason our planning notes should identify priority items that must be pursued if the interview threatens to be briefer than we had anticipated. And for this reason we should request the possibility of returning.

We should also ask whether the respondent knows of other people we ought to see, and in sensitive subject areas (especially policy research) we should appreciate hints about who *not* to see, for the unsympathetic can make access to others difficult. If we are with a partner, the leader should ask the partner if he or she has any further questions. We should ask the respondent if there are any points that he or she would like to clarify or emphasize. Second-hand data (when we are told, for example, what a third party thinks) are as legitimate as direct testimony, for we cannot be sure that what we are told about someone is less true than what they tell us themselves. It is useful, therefore, to ask a researcher what someone else thinks. And I often ask, finally, "Given the subject we have been discussing, is there anything you think I should have asked or that I have neglected?" Responses to this question can be surprisingly useful. No matter how unsuccessful or disagreeable the interview may have been, gratitude for time and trouble should be expressed clearly, and every effort should be made to depart on congenial terms.

After the Interview

Immediately after an interview we must find a place (perhaps a nearby café, or in summer a nearby park bench) where we can spend approximately an hour with our notes. Even if a tape recorder was not used during the interview, it may now prove useful for pouring out our thoughts. All points should be clarified. Memory should be purged. All full statements that may be quoted later should be written out. Questions should be checked to see if everything was satisfactorily answered, and we should be sure all answers were recorded. As we become more experienced, this exercise becomes less time-consuming, but no matter how experienced we are, we must devote some time for this purpose.

*   *   *

There are a number of further concerns surrounding interviewing and pursuing research that we must now consider. For one thing, we have not yet discussed how to organize a work schedule; for another, we need to consider how to maintain our data. In Chapter 4 we will address these matters and a number of other peculiar field problems, such as gaining access to people in bureaucracies, and what we need to consider when the research is completed and we are ready to go home.

Notes

1. See my discussion of related problems in "An Antidote for Apology, Service and Witchcraft in Policy Analysis," in Phillip Gregg, *Problems of Theory in Policy Analysis* (Lexington, Mass: Lexington Books, 1976).

2. William F. Whyte, *Street Corner Society: The Social Structure of an Italian Slum* (Chicago: University of Chicago Press, 1955).

3. Elliot Liebow, *Tally's Corner: A Study of Negro Streetcorner Men* (Boston: Little, Brown and Co., 1967).

4. Edgar Morin, *The Red and the White: Report from a French Vil-*

lage, translated by A. M. Sheridan-Smith (New York: Pantheon Books, 1970).

5. Laurence Wylie, *Village in the Vaucluse* (Cambridge, Mass.: Harvard University Press, 1954); and Laurence Wylie, ed., *Chanzeaux: A Village in Anjou* (Cambridge, Mass.: Harvard University Press, 1966).

6. See the results of such inquiry in Elliot J. Feldman and Lily Gardner Feldman, "The Special Relationship Between Canada and the United States," *Jerusalem Journal of International Relations* 4, no. 4 (June 1980), pp. 56–85.

4

Organizing and Managing Field Research

Field research involves so many unexpected events that it is extremely difficult to organize a routine. Nevertheless, it is important to develop one so that data are well preserved and we do not slide into the idleness that can result from unstructured and undisciplined work.

Structuring Your Day

Let us consider how we might organize a "typical" day of field research. We have already discussed the actual conduct of research, but we have not placed those activities in the context of a work day. How do we get to an interview? How many interviews can we do in a day? What should we do with the time between interviews? And what happens when the last interview of the day is completed?

As I mentioned earlier, it is important not to be late for appointments. In cities such as London and Paris it is difficult to know how long it will take to reach a certain address. The Metro might break down; a bus might be caught in traffic. Our first rule, then, is to allow more time than we think conceivably necessary. We cannot overcome natural disaster, but we can anticipate natural conditions to some extent at least. If all goes smoothly and we arrive well in advance, we can sit in the car or find a café or bar in which to wait. We should not, because we are early, seek an early entry to the appointment. We should be on time. However, we might occasionally arrive for an interview in a residential neighborhood by bus or taxi in a driving rain one-half hour early. There is no café or bar or shop. There are only private residences, pavement, and rain. This situation is the exception—we will have to ring the doorbell. But conditions should be this extreme.

The distance between interviews will determine how many interviews can be managed in a given day. In rural America it may be possible, traveling by car, to cover seventy-five miles and conduct as many as six interviews between 8:30 A.M. and 10:00 P.M. But in London during the same time period, three interviews may be the most possible. Let us consider some of the constraints.

Unless interviews are in the same neighborhood, at least one-half hour must be allowed for travel. If the location of an interview is unfamiliar, another half hour must be allowed for getting lost. A minimum of one and one-half hours must be allowed for the interview itself, for the respondent may be delayed or late or sufficiently open that the interview extends beyond anticipated limits (a standard interview length is one hour). And one hour must be allowed for memory "purge." Thus, from the time we leave home to the time we arrive at the second interview in another neighborhood we have had to allow a minimum of three and one-half hours. Barring loss of way and excessive delays, if we leave home at 8:00 A.M. we can begin a second interview no earlier than 11:30 (experience will shorten the "purge" time, which may also eventually be consolidated with travel between appointments, but at most one full hour could be saved). If we are working in the same neighborhood, of course, much time is saved, and more work is possible.

As a rule, if we have an interview scheduled to follow one just conducted, we should travel to the site of the second interview before going through our notes. This way we remove the anxiety of having to get to the next place while trying to concentrate on the previous interview. But in any event, we should allow reasonable time between appointments.

There are few people in Europe, especially on the official level, whom we will be able to see earlier than 9:00 A.M. (in England, earlier than 10:00 A.M.). Furthermore, unless we have a luncheon appointment, we will not be able to see anyone between 11:30 A.M. and 2:30 or 3:00 P.M. Thus, we may only be able to manage one appointment in the morning, with possibly a second over lunch. Luncheon appointments, moreover, may take the entire lunch period, which means that when the hour's "purge" is counted in, an afternoon appointment could not begin before 4:00 or 4:30. Obviously, except possibly for dinner or evening, a 4:00 appointment will be the last of the day. Finally, due to the nature of a European dinner, no appointment can be planned for after dinner. The most complete possible day in a European city (and these points apply almost equally to the countryside) will consist of appointments in the morning, over lunch, in the afternoon, and over dinner. More probably and normally, however, interviews will be scheduled only in the morning and in the afternoon. If we see more than one person in the same building or in the same organization, we can accomplish more. Otherwise, these are the limits.

It is possible to do more in the United States or Canada for several reasons: Meals are less formal and time-consuming; offices open earlier in the morning and stay open through the lunch hours; adjustments in schedule can be made more easily over the telephone, with last-minute luncheon dates normal—in sharp contrast to what would normally be possible in Europe. In any event, we must be aware of the occurrences in a day that will take sizeable periods of time. And we must remember that interviewing can be both exhilarating and exhausting. Several interviews in one day ultimately prove counterproductive in terms of our own sharpness and receptiveness and may render us less than effective the next day.

Having our own car is indispensable in rural areas and advantageous even in cities. We can more readily carry a tape recorder, extra batteries, tapes, notes, etc., and we can more readily control our own travel time. In traffic-congested urban centers, public transportation may be faster, but our own car may be more reliable. And although impoverished researchers do not imagine themselves the users of taxis, we must be prepared to hail a taxi if we have no car and we must reach an appointment.

Our days can also be organized around the use of archives, or we can plan to spend the morning in a library and the afternoon conducting an interview. However we organize in this regard, we must remember to leave time to prepare interviews, not merely to conduct them. That is, we must track down public statements, personal histories, and so forth, and we must prepare questions both for full, methodical interviews and for interviews that may unexpectedly be cut short.

I mentioned earlier that we should arrange interviews by writing letters. Unfortunately, we usually have to write a number of letters at the same time for interviews to be conducted during the same period. Once the letters have been sent we wait in dread that nine people are all eager to see us for lunch on the same day. Rarely, in fact, do serious conflicts arise, but frequently we may be forced to set up more appointments in a given day than we might have wished while leaving other days free. One rule might be followed here: It is better to lose one interview entirely than to jeopardize the quality of two or three in an effort to squeeze too many into too little time.

After the Day's Work

If we are studying citizen groups or trade unions, we are likely to attend a fair number of evening meetings. Other objects generally do not require this particular demand on our time, however. We may decide to reserve the evenings for ourselves, but we must also remember that other important activities related to the day's work ought to be undertaken then.

Every interview requires a thank-you note. If we intend to see someone again, we might time the note to arrive a couple of weeks before we renew contact for another meeting. This method reminds the respondent who we are while extending a positive impression. The note might also be sent as we near the end of our field work, whereupon we might be able to write more personally about how the interview fit into our overall work. In general, however, it is probably best to write a note soon after the interview. If our notes reveal further brief questions or points yet needing clarification, we can request written answers at the same time that we express thanks for the interview. If materials are sent by the respondent after an interview, a note is also required. Evenings are a good time for this activity.

Project data should be maintained in at least three organized files, the development of which is a daily (or regular evening) task. First, we should maintain a file of contacts. We should list each person we see, their address, official position, where and when we saw them, and a few notes, perhaps, about our impressions of them. We should list how we came to see them (Did someone else make the contact for us? Did someone else recommend this person?) and whether it was agreed we could see them again. From our notes of the day, we should add to our contact file all names, addresses, and other pertinent information concerning other people recommended by the people we have interviewed that day.

After we have completed the contact file for the day, we should file and catalogue all documents and written materials we have collected. There almost always comes a point when we discover ourselves being offered materials we already have. If we have not catalogued, we are liable not to realize we already possess something. It is better to have more than less, but it is also better not to clutter our data with extra copies of the same documents. Also, if our field research relies more on collecting documents than on interviews, it is essential that we organize what we have collected. Not only should we catalogue generally, but we should examine the document to have an idea what it contains. There is a tendency in field research to collect documents and then examine them when we leave the field. If time allows, this tendency should be avoided. For one thing, documents may provide information that we might, if ignorant, try to uncover in interviews. For another thing, the documents may point us in important directions that would be impossible to pursue once we have left the field.

The third file we should maintain contains the interviews themselves. We should take our notes from the day and write them up in detail. For interviews we have taped, we should make an index of what the interview covers. These complete reports will likely be our principal data when the time to analyze and write up our results finally comes. Therefore, although again there is a tendency after a long and tiring day not to bother with these activities, it is crucial that we push ourselves. If we establish a routine of completing these files every day, the perception that they are an unnecessary bother will begin to fade.

In addition to these formal files, it is helpful to keep a notebook with us at all times in which we can record anything that occurs to us. As we get involved in the research, ideas will spark when we least expect them. We need a place to record these ideas, or we will later discover ourselves with countless little bits of paper, relatively useless. Some ideas may seem absurd or irrelevant at the time; we should record them anyway. When we write up results, we should refer to this notebook, for it may well lead us down the most profitable analytical paths. And before we leave the field we should consult this notebook; it may remind us of things needing to be completed. Finally, although the notebook need not become a diary, each evening we should consider—on a routine basis—whether something struck us during the day. If any thought or line of reasoning occurs to us, we should record it in this special notebook.

The special notebook may be of greatest use when we think we are stuck and have lost our way. Research is easily derailed by broken appointments, data that do not correspond at all to hypotheses, or simply lack of cooperation from many people. At such times we should look to this notebook and write ourselves memoranda: What are we trying to find out? What have we learned so far? What are the unanswered questions? Reflect on the objects in the hypotheses. Have we explored all of them? Writing out answers to such questions can get us back on track.

Every researcher will organize materials to suit personal preference. Some people like file cards, others notebooks, and so on. Although we should choose on the basis of our personal preferences, we should be guided by the facts that (1) materials need to be carried easily and perhaps frequently; and (2) our notes may be consulted by others.

Bureaucracies and Hard-to-Get Information

I wish to make a few brief remarks about getting to see the right person in a bureaucracy and getting information that seems inaccessible. There is one principle that governs both problems: We should try to go around instead of through the obstacles.

Buildings that house administrators have countless obstacles, usually human. In Italy there is likely to be a porter at the front door, at the end of every hallway, perhaps near every elevator entrance. In England there will be a guard at the front door; these guards are usually more efficient than the Italian porters and will not let a visitor past without authorization. For this reason it is hazardous just to show up saying, "I would like to see someone who can tell me about . . ." One solution to this problem, when in fact we do not know what branch of the particular bureaucracy will have an answer for us, is to begin with the telephone. We can let the switchboard operator route us through the organization until, as we keep saying, "Yes, that's right," we are given the name of the department we want and perhaps even the name of the responsible person there. Then we can show up at the door and announce that we are going to this or that department or to see this or that person. It is best if we can tell the guard we have an appointment, but we should be careful not to lie; the guard will probably telephone upstairs to check. And through our conversations on the telephone we should be sure to get names. We should never end a conversation with a bureaucrat without knowing to whom we have spoken.

Although more manpower will be distributed to block our path in the Italian system, the greater number of people generally proves a far less formidable obstacle than the English guards. The important rule is not to talk with anyone stationed outside an office and never to hesitate or seem uncertain of where we are going when we are in public view. There should be no hesitation at the front door. We must enter directly, perhaps extending a warm and familiar "good morning" or "good afternoon"—in the native language—to the guard. We should make our way directly to stairs or elevators without hesitating. A second rule is that, unless we are studying office personnel, low-level bureaucrats, or staff, there is no one on the lower floors of a multistoried building whom we want to see. Decision makers and authorities, like the aristocrats of old, ascend to the high places and tend to occupy offices on the upper floors. We want to get to the upper floors, therefore, before someone detains us.

Almost every building will have a general directory on the first floor. However, every floor should have a directory as well, or at least names on doors. Therefore, we should tend to consult directories on the upper floors instead of below. And we should remember that, whereas it is the job of the guards to block us, secretaries have no similar task. Here is someone we can usually ask. A courteous inquiry will often produce a courteous and helpful reply. Once in the office area, a secretary may guide us to our desired destination. Moreover, it is better to ask secretaries than officials as they pass in the corridors. The latter will direct us to the guards or, worse, question our presence. The secretaries probably will not.

People who work in bureaucracies are often hard to locate. Bureaucracies also contain information that the staff may be reluctant to share. Public records, we may be told, are not public because they are too disorganized. In England, each ministry of state has its own library, and we can often find material there. But in Italy, for example, we may not find libraries and we may find a pattern of secrecy that seems to make everything pertinent unavailable. One solution to this problem is the corollary of our description of entering buildings: Go to the top. Another rule is never to waste time negotiating with someone at a level where the materials are kept but where release of them to the "wrong" people could bring severe internal retribution. We should seek permission from above for nonsensitive materials.

Sensitive materials, of course, are another matter: For these we must try the lower echelons first and hope to find either a disgruntled worker or someone who will make a mistake. If we were to begin above, we might generate a proclamation that would seal off all materials definitively. We must always remember that relationships within bureaucracies are hierarchical and continue after the episode of our visit passes. Those in the upper echelons have a stake in being regarded as superior by those below. That means that those above are always prepared to contravene what has already occurred below. If below we are denied something, those above may order it opened. Unfortunately, the reverse is also true, though probably less frequent.

When the way is blocked above and below, we can only seek the help of others inside or outside the bureaucracy. One idea is to look for someone no longer working there who might have friends or who might have kept materials. Secretaries also can prove remarkably helpful sometimes. In each instance where the way seems blocked, we must try another way before bulldozing straight ahead. That said, we should sometimes be prepared, as a last resort, to bulldoze. We need only say we are about to publish and that their side of the story, given the paucity of information available, is not very favorable. Such a veiled threat, after repeated efforts to secure help, can sometimes produce wonders.

Bureaucracies are not alone in making materials difficult to obtain. One other pertinent case that is an especially frequent impediment to young historians involves access already granted to some senior scholar. The senior scholar may, in turn, assert exclusive access. If we want the materials for the same purpose as the person who has exclusive access, there is not much we can do. If, however, our research merely intersects over these materials and we want them for different purposes, we need to appeal both to those who have granted the rights and to those who hold the rights, emphasizing the special need we have. We can employ the journalistic tactics I have already noted with regard to getting interviews. Finally, we can threaten to publish the fact that another scholar is blocking access to important research materials for apparently selfish purposes. Usually materials can be pried loose from their most selfish guardians if access has already been granted to someone.

Hanging around a bureaucracy or an organization or meeting people casually in a cafeteria or at evening meetings (of, say, a citizens' group) can make a face familiar and, eventually, more welcome. There is a high risk in overexposure, but when direct efforts fail, the subtler but equally eager approaches can be fruitful.

Team Research

Most of our discussion has assumed that we are working alone. Although thesis research will be independent, other research often involves teams. When teams work in the field, there are a number of rules to follow.

First, the team must have some place where all members pass every day. Ideally the team will share an apartment or a house. If it is not possible to arrange accommodations this way, then a common office is desirable. At the very least, all members of the team must be in daily contact with one another.

There are many reasons for following this rule. Although each member of a team may have a separate assignment, data that will serve more than one person often can be found in the same place. It is always preferable for one person to collect the pertinent data that can serve two. Thus, if more than one researcher seeks information in a provincial office, it is best if everyone provides a single researcher with all requests for the provincial office.

As another example, the same person might be the potential respondent to two different interviews. Where two members of a team want to interview the same person, they should either organize and conduct the interview together, or one person should conduct the interview in behalf of the team. Only under extreme circumstances should more than one interview of the same person be conducted by different members of the same team on closely related topics.

To avoid the embarrassment of unwittingly harrassing the same person through separate contacts for separate appointments, a research team ideally should meet every evening—perhaps over dinner—to discuss contacts and the next day's research plans. When letters are to be sent requesting interviews, all team members should be informed so that each has an opportunity to indicate whether a given person appears on two lists. Only one letter should go to that person. A research team needs to avoid the pitfall of becoming its own bureaucracy.

For the best coordination of a research team there must be a leader. The leader assumes responsibility for guaranteeing regular contact among the members and for avoiding multiple interview contacts. The leader should also coordinate data collection so that each trip to a place by a member of the team is profitable to everyone concerned. Thus, in the review of the next day's plans, each member of the team should report on what they will do, whom they will see, and what exactly they will seek. Each member must then be sure to ask every other member if a given trip can be of mutual service.

Research teams also need to avoid the tendency to fall into mutual dependencies. If there are four team members working approximately forty hours per week, there will then be one hundred sixty working hours. If the team tends to interview in pairs, however, then the time that could have been spent in independent data collection begins to lose value. Ideally the team will be composed of individuals with independent assignments closely related. Sometimes these assignments will require team interviewing; more often they should involve independent work serving more than one of the team's interests.

Combining Personal Life with Field Research

Field research can become all-consuming, but (as with all activities) complete devotion to it is not necessarily healthy. If field research is being conducted in a strange environment, however, there may be many constraints on leading a normal social life.

The greatest intellectual problem involves the degree of contact possible with people being studied. Anthropologists seek such contact, and the "participant-observer" school of sociology encourages it. For examining the internal dynamics of single groups or populations there is probably nothing better than participant-observation—sharing responsibility while watching closely all the actors. However, if we are studying conflict between or among groups, institutions, or individuals, contact may compromise our independence. If we frequently socialize with one group, we may begin, unconsciously, to lean to its side. Even if we resist this tendency, a competitive group may perceive that we are leaning this way and refuse to deal with us or prove less than cooperative. We are especially inclined to the side of one party when that party treats us very well and the other party treats us badly. We are then inclined to ask ourselves, "Why not return their invitation?" The answer must lie in the purpose of our research.

If we hope to know all we can about a group of people—be it

a trade union or a board of trustees—the best possible way to accomplish our objective is through frequent and varied contact. Thus, we should seek contact whenever there is an opportunity. If, on the other hand, we are studying relations between the trade union and the board of trustees, inviting the chairman of the board home to dinner is not likely to help much with the trade union. And if we think all will be satisfactory as long as we have the union leader in the next evening, we need to consider what they will surely consider: Who was invited first? In short, if we choose to integrate our social lives with the social lives of our respondents, we must appreciate that there is a strong and inescapable political content in our choice.

Our greatest problem in this regard is to avoid becoming identified with one side of a conflict or with one group of people. We do not want to be drawn into the conflict itself, nor do we want to incur anyone's hostility. In general, therefore, we must be reticent about extending invitations ourselves and cautious about accepting those of others. Even when studying the union, we risk becoming ensnared in an internal conflict by being identified with a faction or with certain individuals.

There are three main reasons why these constraints are particularly painful to confront. For one thing, we derive a much greater sense of satisfaction out of meeting the people we are studying informally as well as formally; we sense that we understand and know them better when we deal with them on a more personal level. For another thing, we find ourselves in strange settings where our only human contact may be with the people we are studying. Not only is it alienating to convert people into objects of observation, but it is isolating if we see only people with whom we must maintain formal relations. Finally, as we cut off our own social lives, we tend to cut off the social lives of family members who may accompany us. The social and personal alienation faced by a researcher may therefore be more serious for a spouse or for children. They may have no professional activity available, and they also find themselves in a strange setting. They are probably less equipped to adapt to the new environment because of language deficiency (not having been trained for this work or place), and they may be asked to limit their social contacts because we worry about being compromised.

All these problems are greatest in small communities where we feel greater pressure to socialize with the same people we are studying because the apparent alternative is loneliness. In urban settings we can perhaps find other company. We cannot set down absolute rules concerning social contact. But, again recognizing that the lack of social contact is fundamentally alienating, we must try to consider our professional and personal needs separately. We must recognize that social contact must be weighed in terms of the purpose of our study. It is perhaps cynical to pursue social contact merely to help collect data, but field research is a special, not a normal, condition of our lives. And it is at least realistic to recognize that although our motive may be innocent, it can still bring on damaging consequences.

Once these risks and constraints are understood, we must then, as always, make our own choices. Extended, isolated field research has risks not only for the research, but also for our own mental stability. If we are reduced to a choice between the two, then we must risk some feature of our research in behalf of our mental health. But perhaps being aware of the dangers in advance can reduce the risk of such a choice being forced upon us.

One way or another we will have to make our way in the community where we are conducting our study. Thus, it is perhaps wisest to seek social contact deliberately with people unrelated to our research as early as possible. Such contact can serve to reduce the problems that may develop later on. We must not forget our own personal needs, for they will not forget us. In the end, the success or failure of a project may depend on whether we have been able to make ourselves comfortable enough to pursue our research effectively.

Finishing and Going Home

We never really finish field research. There are always more people to see, more questions to ask, more material to collect. However, we cannot go on forever. Knowing when we have enough data is largely intuitive. For example, we may collect a whole new version of a given event each time we speak to someone, but at some point we must say simply, "I have enough versions to get the idea." Often we will have to approximate a story and assume we have enough information.

We stop collecting data when (1) we run out of money; (2) we have to meet a publication or contract deadline; (3) we run out of time; or (4) we run out of patience. At any of these points, the research is not really finished; rather, the research ends. Perhaps we sense diminishing returns, perhaps we don't, but at some point we must stop and depend upon what we have already collected. The study will be a snapshot of events and opinions and perspectives and documents of a moment in time. We cannot expect more from the data, and we cannot do more ourselves. At that point we collect our things to go home. And if we are home already, we halt the field work and begin the systematic analysis of the data collected.

Finally, let me mention a couple of important considerations about moving after the completion of field research away from home. If we plan to travel by car, bus, train, or boat, there is perhaps no problem in carrying the fruits of our labors with us. But if we fly, or if we need to carry suitcases of clothing and other possessions on some other form of public transportation, then we must separate ourselves from our data. There are three partial solutions to this potential problem.

The most irreplaceable materials, such as contact lists, interview reports, and secret documents, should be separated from the other materials. If at all possible, these materials should be kept with us at all times. Thus, if we are flying, we should plan to carry these materials on board. We should recognize, however, that they will probably be heavy and that someone at the airline may oppose our refusal to check the bag in. To mitigate some of the potential calamity in such a confrontation, the airline representative should be told that we have research materials—the products of months or years of work—from which we do not intend to be parted. Whatever arrangement need be made, we shall declare, we must carry this baggage on. We should plan, at the same time, to be relatively unburdened of other carry-on things so as to reduce any clamor over this particular bag.

Replaceable materials can be mailed, shipped, or flown, either as extra luggage or air freight. If we choose the mails, we should send two separate packages with everything duplicated.

This way we double the expense but significantly multiply the probability that we will see our materials again. We also need to pack well; scrambled computer cards in a mail sack are as good as lost. And if at all possible, we should avoid putting materials on boats. Final shipping costs, when we finish with forwarding agents, packers, etc., will not be significantly less than air freight costs would have been, and since there is much less handling by air freight, there is much less risk of pilferage or loss. Furthermore, we can send papers as air freight or as extra baggage on the same plane that we are traveling on and greet the data at the other end. The carrying capacity of jumbo aircraft has reduced significantly the cost of such shipping. The material we have collected is simply too valuable to take any unnecessary risk. We should pack accordingly.

Getting our data safely home is the last field aspect of a field research project, and perhaps the most important single task we face. When successful, we can proceed to produce the results of our work; when unsuccessful, there is nothing to be said—and perhaps nothing to be done.

A Final Word

We have now considered most of the more important aspects of field research in the social sciences. This little guide has advised on formulating research tasks, selecting appropriate methods for pursuing them, organizing strategies for overcoming research obstacles, and structuring time and effort in the conduct of field research. It has warned of pitfalls while, it is hoped, encouraging adventure. It may be both useful in the field as a reminder and useful for preparing your study before going into the field. With the companionship of these tips and the experience that has led to them, students will perhaps make fewer mistakes and suffer less anxiety. Most of what I have warned about, after all, I know because I was not warned myself and had to learn through often painful experience. I have stood in the rain waiting for appointments without an umbrella, arrived at incorrect addresses, forgotten to press the record button of a tape recorder, carried too few pens with ink, and lost irreplaceable data in the international mails. I have seen others depend for years on access to resources that will never be opened, receive mail sacks of scrambled computer cards, forget crucial personal details of someone they are interviewing, and miss appointments because of failed public transportation. Research ought not to be painful. This guide is intended to help relieve some of the pain—or at least some of the anxiety—and thereby increase the many pleasures.

Appendix: An Illustrative Interview

Good interviewing technique comes with practice, with experience, and with reflection on why interviews succeed or fail. The annotated and edited transcript that follows should provide insight into the actual conduct of an interview and into how and why valuable answers—revealing sometimes new and startling information long after events have passed—can be elicited.

The respondent in this interview, Max Lejeune, was chosen because of his particular experience, expertise, and position of responsibility. The interview was organized around questions of fact as well as opinion and aimed, above all, at bringing out attitudes and perceptions on central questions of policy:

- How did a Socialist government minister responsible for the policies governing the armed forces of France in Algeria reconcile his socialism with the colonial objectives of the war?
- How did he perceive the enemy? Was their terror different from the later terror of the OAS?
- How did he distinguish the Algerian experience from the recently terminated war in Indochina? How was the 1956 Suez invasion related to French military efforts in Algeria?
- What did he understand to be the role of the French nation, and what were the relationships between the nation and the army and the army and the Algerians?
- What lessons from the war in Algeria were learned about

the army and the nation? What is the utility of an army now, and what is the utility of conscripts?

The main objective of the interview was to explore the perceptions of the responsible government minister and to establish whether the consequences of sending French conscripts (the *contingent*) were understood in advance. A second objective was to establish the strategic perceptions of the government and, hence, the role of the army in Indochina, Algeria, and Suez. As a third objective, I sought to clarify the French definition of the national obligation for military service through the specific experience of Algeria. Similar questions, with similar purposes, were put to a number of other prominent participants in this period of French decision making, including Robert Lacoste, Jacques Soustelle, Christian Pineau, Maurice Bourgès-Maunoury, and General André Zeller.

Max Lejeune was secretary of state for the armed forces in France from 1948 to 1950 and in 1956-57. He was also president of the National Defense Commission of the National Assembly during 1954-55 and vice president of the National Assembly in 1947-48, 1967-68, and 1970-71. During 1956-57 he bore direct responsibility for the decision to send the *contingent* to fight in Algeria.

This interview with Max Lejeune was conducted at the Assemblée Nationale in Paris on April 28, 1971. He warned at the outset that the interview could last no more than thirty to forty-five minutes. The transcript here was prepared from a tape recording in French by Leonie Gordon and edited from our sixty-minute discussion.

<u>Comments</u>

<u>Interview Transcript</u>

ML: I can give you a half-hour or three-
quarters--no more.

EJF: I will try to be direct and to the
point. I would like to begin with this
question: when it was decided to send the
contingent in March 1956, the decision was
taken, if I understand correctly, because
it was thought necessary to establish a
French military presence throughout Algeria?

ML: Yes, the decision was taken because in
France, at that time, we considered Algeria
three departments of France. We sent the
soldiers of the contingent there because it
was France. In contrast, we did not send the
contingent to Indochina because Indochina
was a protectorate, not a state of the French
Republic.

No conscripts to Indochina
an important difference
between France and the U.S.
He raised the point here;
pursue it right away, even
though it comes later on
my list.

EJF: But, at the time of Dienbienphu, did not
one say, "Perhaps we must send one Frenchman
to come to the aid of another?" Even at that
time was it not possible to send the contingent?

ML: No, it was impossible. They thought, at
the time, of sending volunteers from the contingent, but it was absolutely impractical for
the military administration.

"Absolutely" means move on;
he also said, in the first
question, that Algeria was
a French <u>domestic</u> problem.
How domestic?

EJF: Do you believe, in that case, that
one can use the army domestically? For
example, there was much talk during May
1968; might it have been possible, at
that time, to use the army, say, to stop
the strike?

ML: ll, in 1948-49 there were general
st   s, and as the Minister of the period
said, they could have become insurrectional;

the army was used to confront the danger
and to maintain order in the northern
departments and in Pas de Calais.

EJF: So you think Algeria was to be treated
in the same way, just as if it were metro-
politan France?

ML: Algeria? Yes, yes. Because, according
to military regulations one mission of the
army is not only to defend the integrity of
the national territory, but also to assure
the maintenance of public order.

EJF: You introduced a system of rotation
for the contingent in Algeria, in a sense
seeking to assure equal service for everyone
by requiring everyone to do a tour of service
there.

ML: Yes.

EJF: Did you mean truly to involve <u>all</u>
the nation in Algeria through this involvement of the contingent?

ML: Yes. We did not want only the presence of a professional army, which would
have given the impression of a colonial
war. Algeria was part of France, because
the definition of a nation is not racial.

He is convinced Algeria was   EJF: After some time in Algeria the
a domestic problem; no use   generals complained about the contingent,
debating the point more.   the conscripts....*

                               ML: Not at all.

They most certainly did;   EJF: You don't think so?
how far will he go with   ML: Not at all.
this disclaimer?   EJF: That is to say that...

                               ML: When I was Secretary of State for
Military Affairs in Algeria I spent over
eighteen months, during which 10-12 days of
every month were devoted to visiting every

soldier. At no time did general officers
complain about the attitude of their men.
Just the contrary.

EJF: OK.

ML: There was nothing comparable, even at
the worst moments, to what seems to be
taking place now in Vietnam with American
conscripts.

Press a specific instance.

EJF: In April 1961, nonetheless, the
contingent went on strike....

ML: But in April 1961 it was because the
French Government changed its policy.
General de Gaulle declared that Algeria
was to be Algerian, so young soldiers said,
"So, what do we do now? Why should we risk
our lives if the leader of France says
'Algeria for the Algerians'?" To the contrary,
for these young guys they said, "It is
finished."

**There was a strong insur-
rectionist movement within
the contingent seeking to
end the war; will he admit
it?**

EJF: But you believe, then, that they simply
followed General de Gaulle, and it was not
something else affecting their decision to
strike?

ML: No. They were scared, especially of
following the military chiefs who wanted to
maintain the former policy of a French
Algeria. Naturally, they followed the
government, but they did so as boys of 20
and 21 years old. I would like very much
to be able to say that they thought, "It is
the law we must follow," of course. But for
most the truth is they realized their own
lives were at risk.

**His view is clear; what,
then, was the military
strategy? Quote him.**

EJF: In 1956 you said, for example,
"Hundreds of thousands of men will not
suffer," and you insisted that the army's
problem in peacekeeping in Algeria required

* NOTE: Ellipses indicate
editing in the tape.

a change of habits.

ML: A change of methods.

EJF: But do you believe, then, that this task was accomplished?

ML: We were involved, always, in a rebellion of people who were prisoners in Indochina, in the Vietnamese camps of political propaganda with the Vietminh; they returned to Algeria after the Geneva accords had ended the Vietnam War. I said to President René Coty that it was absolutely indispensable to end the affair very quickly, to do so by exceptional means, not of a massive military force but by severe and swift police tactics.

EJF: M. Lacoste, at the same time, wanted the infusion of some 100,000 men....

ML: When I arrived on the scene in 1956 I did not want an immediate increase in the number of men. I asked only that the methods be changed. M. Lacoste, however, demanded a French presence in Algeria through the use of the contingent; I was not in favor, but I went along out of party solidarity. When there are military forces in a country, despite everything the local population very quickly feels the weight of this presence, which can degrade the climate, the atmosphere. For this reason I understood very well when you said, "In sending the soldiers of the contingent to spread out through Algeria you implied that France intended to stay," but at the same time it is important to create illusions. One accentuates the weight of the military presence on people who have their own civilian problems. Naturally, the army provided many services, building roads,

> Show you know the facts and the personalities so that he cannot simply change the subject.

> He has indeed understood me; and he has begun to explain more.

teaching children, managing civilian administration which did not exist before, but it
was no less true that it was necessary to
separate the promoters of rebellion from the
life of the state as quickly as possible.

Fighting a rebellion through road construction? That wasn't his policy.

EJF: Do you think this civilian role for the
army is proper? Does it always exist for
an army?

ML: No, it does not always exist....The
directives given General Challe, to apply

For a period Challe conducted a conventional war.

firm military force, were dictated by me in
1956. I was attacked, of course, by certain
communist newspapers, but I had a mission to
accomplish, and I defined it at the time
as the mission undertaken by General Challe--
which led to the pacification when, to the
army's great surprise, General de Gaulle
decided to deal with the leaders of the
rebellion when they pleaded for peace.

So much for his military preferences; what of military politics? Begin with specific case.

EJF: Could you tell me something about the
resignation of General Guillaume in 1956?
ML: General Guillaume was a problem that
involved M. Bourgès-Maunoury, who was Minister
for National Defense, more than me.

(...I know you were both involved.)

EJF: Yes, but...
ML: Because General Guillaume at the time,
if I recall correctly, was in Morocco. It
was another problem, not precisely military....
EJF: A political problem?
ML: Yes.
EJF: Could you...

He really does not want to answer. Return to his perception of the war.

ML: You know, my memories are quite fluid.
If I had the time to look at my notes from
the period I would say, but I fear going back
too far beyond what I remember and I do not
want to give you a wholly personal and superficial impression.

EJF: I understand. You described the enemy at the outset of problems in Algeria in very specific terms--that they were assassins, fanatics....

ML: I said it and I take none of it back. I still think it.

Does he object to terror or to the rejection of his plan for a French Algeria?

EJF: How would you like to describe, then, the terror of the OAS that followed, for they seem quite similar to me?

ML: Don't you see? I am a socialist who, as early as 1936, supported French citizenship for the moslems in Algeria....It is important to understand that I was, in 1958, alongside General de Gaulle when he said, "Long live French Algeria." He descended from the podium and said to me, "So, Lejeune."

("I felt personally betrayed and still do....")

"Oh, my general, you have called for a French Algeria. That means integration. Hurry to do it. It is possible, but you must hurry." I myself continued to believe in my own formula of Algeria within the Republic. This cry of "Long live Algeria," the famous "I have understood you," all that--the French recorded that, the Europeans of French Algeria, with eight years of formal conflict and you must then understand that for them there was immense disillusionment when General de Gaulle abandoned this policy. And for the army, there was anger, for they were asked suddenly to play a different part. To protect France, this army thought, it would now be necessary to control and manage themselves, for they had been betrayed. One should never involve an army in political activity; yet, from the moment they were involved, above all by someone like General de Gaulle--with the prestige he enjoyed in the army--they sensed the betrayal.

Obviously he thinks they're
different, but make him
draw a clear distinction.

EJF: Do you believe, then, that these
activities were similar, the acts of terror
driven by the same political rationale for
the OAS as for the FLN?

He sees the point; he also
sees the political awkward-
ness of his opposition to
ultimate French policy.

ML: There was at the time, in France and in
Algeria, provocation. It is very delicate
for me to deal with this question with you....
The terror of the OAS was a reaction against
those who appeared to abandon the French cause.
I do not justify it, but there is this senti-
ment, that the army was repressed. It is
necessary to speak of the terror of the FLN.

He still leaves open my
question; try one last time.

What is dramatic for armies is the violence--
violence engenders hate, and hate engenders
more hate.

EJF: That is exactly what I am asking. I
would like to know whether you wish to
differentiate between the reasons on each
side for apparently similar acts. That is
precisely the question.

ML: I hold responsible for all that those
who failed to keep their involvement with
an eye for the interests of the country.
Voilà.

Let him continue; he is now
telling his cosmic view of
the war's relationship to
the destiny of France.

EJF: OK.

ML: For me, the guy responsible is General
de Gaulle. I wrote him, fifteen days before
he died when he sent me a copy of his book,
dedicated to me. I thanked him for the book,
but I told him the reading of it gave me
enormous pain because when he came to power
those who helped him get there--the French
people--expected a guarantee of domestic peace.
I insisted that the policies he followed returned France to a hexagon, no longer the great
power for which he had hoped himself, having
lost access to Saharan oil--which meant the

loss of France's energy independence. General
de Gaulle perhaps counted greatly on the more
rapid development of nuclear reactors. He left
France much smaller and much weaker, despite
all appearances.

Was the war not already
lost?

EJF: Do you believe Algeria could have
been retained, even in 1958?

ML: Yes. It is not a matter of keeping
Algeria in the form of French departments.
One could have given it its own evolutive
statute to keep for the long future a common
destiny with France.

EJF: Before May 1958, was your government
on the way to...

ML: Indeed. The special outlined bill
[loi-cadre], it was already before the

I've already interviewed
Soustelle; no utility in
pursuing this line; he
is baiting.

Parliament. And who fought it? M. Soustelle.
I am sure M. Soustelle stayed faithful to his
ideas, but I am obliged to insist that he
fought the bill, and in 1958 General de Gaulle
did not want to take it up again....A minority
of fanatics could not lead me to condemn more
than a million brave Europeans who considered
the place their home.

EJF: This evolution you are talking about--
in what direction were things to evolve?

The concept was never taken
seriously; it is amazing he
still clings to it, but
there is no point in seeking
an explanation here.

ML: I don't see why it was not possible, for
example, for the status of a French union under
the sign of the French Republic--alongside the
metropole and the departments, other territories,
Gabon and the Ivory Coast, for example, which
entered the community.

He still has not clarified
the role of the contingent;
try it again by asking him
to attack his critics (since
he seems to like that).

EJF: There are many critics who think
non-military tasks for the army, and
especially for the contingent, were very
difficult--I'm speaking of psychological
warfare, for example. Do you think the
critics are right?

ML: No, because I would like to say simply
that I like professors when they do psychology and I like military men less when they
try psychology too much. To each his own
mission. There is a tendency to forget the
essential and rudimentary mission of the army.

Don't accept his metaphor-
ical answer; I want some-
thing more specific.

EJF: What do you think, then, really was
possible for the contingent in Algeria?
What could the conscripts accomplish? Were
they to go into battle, to secure areas, or
what exactly?

ML: You know there were conscripts who fell
in Algeria. Of course, there were some. But
it is important too to tell the truth. It was
the special forces, especially paratroopers,
foreign legionnaires, and professional soldiers
who, every time, were in the major operations
in the front lines. That conscripts were
caught in ambushes occasionally, yes. But in
this war, which did witness conscript losses
at unacceptably high levels, we know equally

He never accepted Lacoste's
position and he thinks the
contingent simply got caught
in the line of fire. He sees
no role for them in Algeria
beyond avoiding the appearances of colonial war.

well that an enormous number of these high
losses were attributable to accidents.

EJF: You have said that during the period
in question one preferred well educated and
trained soldiers and that one no longer had
soldiers who simply would follow unexplained
orders. Do you think it is possible to have
an army in which the soldiers are very well

He seems to like the pro-
fessional army; go directly
to the key dilemma.

educated and with whom it is possible to have
something of a dialogue before they follow
orders, an army that does not march solely
on discipline?

ML: Oh, you know, an army without discipline
is not an army. Voilà.

EJF: Can you establish true discipline with

well-educated men?

ML: I don't understand.

EJF: Well, certainly in the traditional army the generals preferred men who would follow orders without question. But when the army is populated by men who question, is it possible for the army to work?

ML: Well, my dear young man, the China of Mao Tse-tung has many admirers, not only intellectuals. If Mao's régime were installed here you would see discipline in work, under arms. It is the weakness of democracy not to accept the necessity of discipline, not only in work, but equally for defense.

EJF: Might I ask a question which might seem tangential to the subject of Algeria? I'd like to know what role Suez played, coming in the midst of the conflict in Algeria. Many people wondered at the time whether entry into the Suez crisis in 1956 would detract from the effort in Algeria, whether there would be enough men to fight, and so forth. Was there a technical or strategic problem in pursuing the Suez invasion at the same time?

ML: During the War in Algeria, you know very well, the rebellion would not have been possible without support from the Arab League and more particularly from Egypt. You know that arms were smuggled across the desert. If hostilities at Suez had not ceased for another ten hours, it would have been the end of Nasser. Paratrooper columns would have entered Cairo and it would have been over. The entire situation in the Middle East would have changed.

EJF: Are you saying that the Suez operation was conceived as part of the Algerian War?

"You can discipline anyone"; the **contingent** can be disciplined. **Move** on.

Yes; OK, was there a
strategic problem?

ML: It is obvious that everything took
place at the same time.

EJF: To pursue the two operations simultaneously, did you require many more troops?

ML: No, no, no. What we had was sufficient.

By all subsequent accounts,
not so; press him with facts.

EJF: But there were only two divisions....

ML: No, no. It would have been all over
when Nasser...when Cairo was reached, it
would have been finished. The Eden-Guy
Mollet conversations during the critical days
were central to the future of the Middle East.

He said "ten"; the point is he
thinks he was betrayed again.
Will he admit the manpower
shortage if I show him where
the troops came from?
Yes, he admits the problem,
but he minimizes it because
of the objective.

What I regret, simply, and I repeat, was that
we did not have another 24-36 hours.

EJF: Do you think NATO was weakened at all
during the invasion when divisions had to be
withdrawn from Germany?

ML: We did not have to withdraw so many men.
With the forces deployed in Egypt--French
units--with the air force and the presence
of massive naval forces in the eastern
Mediterranean--had the affair lasted another
24-36 hours it would have meant the fall of
Nasser, the end of hostilities and for a
moment, at least, the possibility for a total
change of political conditions in the eastern
Mediterranean with a very substantial influence
on events in Algeria.

There ensues a discussion of military involvement in Chad
and the American military effort in Vietnam. Then...

Time is running out; get to
the contemporary questions;
start with an easy confirmation of his credentials.

EJF: You are still a member of the National
Defense Commission....

ML: Yes.

EJF: What do you think of the proposed legal
changes in the law governing national service?

ML: We are generally in agreement for one
year of military service because, unless we

want to collapse--that is, no more military
service....Well, all republicans are still
frightened by the thought of entrusting the
defense of their country to a professional
army. I realize I do not have the right,
given my formal responsibilities, to ignore
technical requirements which today involve
long instruction for handling the new weapons--
and that implies a professional, not a conscript
army--yet the conscript army can be used today
for surface defense of the territory. The real
problem remains, as I have said, that demo-
cracies today are very weak; they do not provide what is necessary, nor the discipline,
for defense.

He is addressing the modern
dilemma; pursue it.

EJF: Then you do not accept that a period of
one year for military service is sufficient
for training an army?

ML: Yes I do, but on condition that the
training is well done. During the last
world war we trained soldiers in six months
and sent them all over. They blended in
with the forces in place. But to extrapolate
from that experience to peacetime--with the
psychological impact of a liberal climate,
individual freedom, leisure time, etc., well.
In wartime, training went from dawn to dusk.
They knew more about military service than
going to the toilet. But we must remember
the difference between service in peacetime
and service in war. For peacetime forces
there must be a popular public respect for a
national defense as necessary and indispensable.

He has said something different, but see how far he might
finally go--probe.

EJF: You think, then, that for defense a
professional army might be better?

ML: I did not say it would be better. It is
obvious, however, that those with the respon-

sibility to govern will be so inclined, for
they will have more confidence in the professional army's technical ability. The army
today is founded on the use of tactical nuclear
weapons; we should be under no illusion that
such use must lead to using the atomic bomb;
then we see that in the last twenty-one years
the character of national defense has changed
brutally.

He won't concede on training, EJF: Then one has reduced effectively the
but perhaps he will on importance of the army, given the dependence
strategy--it led the British on a nuclear strategy.
to abandon conscription. ML: Yes, well, the French government thinks
it has built its defense policy on dissuasion,
with France having an independent capacity.
In any case military service, as presently
conceived, with one year's service and some
peacetime tasks to keep fit, ought to maintain
the accord of democrats and republicans. It
does not exactly provide for the national
defense, but it does not turn over the national
defense simply to a professional army. Nevertheless, I should say that the army has emerged
from the last twelve years profoundly troubled.
Its efforts have been forgotten. It is in
grave condition, a bit like France.

He made the key concession:
compulsory military service is a
political choice whose military
vitality under modern arms and
with present strategy is marginal.
But he is too wedded personally to
the traditional army to pursue this
proposition successfully any further.
He also looks tired and we have gone
much longer than he had offered. Stop here.

EJF: That is a sufficiently pessimistic note; perhaps we should stop. I have no further questions, but perhaps there is something on this subject I have neglected to ask. Is there something else you might want to say, or some ground I have failed to cover?

ML: No, I have spoken freely but I have not had a chance to think of anything I have forgotten to say.

EJF: Are there others you think I should see on some of these subjects?

Good. I have seen them both, which means I am on the right track.

ML: Yes, of course, you should probably talk to M. Soustelle, for example, and M. Pineau for Suez.

EJF: Thank you very much for your generous help. Perhaps I could speak with you again if it seems appropriate?

ML: As you wish.

Much has been learned by inference which must be confirmed by interviewing others and corroborating this testimony with his public statements.

Selected Bibliography

The recommendations here are drawn from several social science disciplines. Anthropologists have been the leading observers of research abroad and of the field experience; sociologists have given the most attention to participant-observation; psychologists have worried most about aspects of interviewing, political scientists about comparisons and evaluation, and so forth.

Many of the works in this bibliography are useful in areas other than the categories in which they have been placed here. The general readers, especially, can be helpful for a variety of purposes, and each has a special utility. Miller's volume, for example, provides guidance in grantsmanship particularly appropriate for sociologists; Murphy offers a useful discussion of elite interviewing, not only for policy evaluators; Barzun and Graff provide very practical guidance for all social science and humanities researchers, not only for historians. On the other hand, one should beware of misleading titles. Shively and Holt and Turner, for example, tend to equate political research with quantitative methods; Wax's account is very personal and lessons often are implicit. Students and scholars should not fear crossing disciplinary lines for practical guidance in using the readings suggested here, however. All address the same means of collecting research data: hearing, reading, and speaking.

General Readers from Disciplinary Perspectives

Barzun, Jacques, and Graff, Henry F. *The Modern Researcher.* New York: Harcourt, Brace and World, 1957. HISTORY

Bickman, Leonard, and Henchy, Thomas. *Beyond the Laboratory: Field Research in Social Psychology.* New York: McGraw-Hill Book Co., 1972. SOCIAL PSYCHOLOGY

Cicourel, Aaron V. *Method and Measurement in Sociology.* Glencoe, Ill.: Free Press, 1964. SOCIOLOGY

Cole, Stephen. *The Sociological Method.* Chicago: Markham, 1972. SOCIOLOGY

Epstein, A. L., ed. *The Craft of Social Anthropology.* London: Tavistock, 1967. ANTHROPOLOGY

Festinger, Leon, and Katz, Daniel, eds. *Research Methods in the Behavioral Sciences.* New York: Holt, Rinehart and Winston, 1966. PSYCHOLOGY and SOCIOLOGY

Forcese, Dennis P., and Richer, Stephen, eds. *Stages of Social Research: Contemporary Perspectives.* Englewood Cliffs, N.J.: Prentice-Hall, 1970. SOCIOLOGY

Glaser, Barney G., and Strauss, Anselm L. *The Discovery of Grounded Theory: Strategies for Qualitative Research.* Chicago: Aldine Press, 1967. SOCIOLOGY

Hammond, Phillip, ed. *Sociologists at Work: Essays on the Craft of Social Research.* New York: Doubleday & Co., 1967. SOCIOLOGY

Jongmans, D. G., and Gutkind, P.C.W., eds. *Anthropologists in the Field.* Assen, Netherlands: Van Gorcum, 1967. ANTHROPOLOGY

Miller, Delbert C. *Handbook of Research Design and Social Measurement.* New York: David McKay Co., 1977. SOCIOLOGY

Powdermaker, Hortense. *Stranger and Friend: The Way of an Anthropologist.* New York: W. W. Norton & Co., 1967. ANTHROPOLOGY

Shiveley, W. Phillips. *The Craft of Political Research.* Englewood Cliffs, N.J.: Prentice-Hall, 1974. POLITICAL SCIENCE

Thomas, D. H. *Figuring Anthropology.* New York: Holt, Rinehart and Winston, 1976. ANTHROPOLOGY

Williams, Thomas R. *Field Methods in the Study of Culture.* New York: Holt, Rinehart and Winston, 1967. ANTHROPOLOGY

Defining Problems

Dubin, Robert. *Theory Building, A Practical Guide to the Construction and Testing of Theoretical Models.* New York: Free Press, 1969.

Kaplan, Abraham. *The Conduct of Inquiry: Methodology for Behavioral Science.* San Francisco: Chandler Publishing, 1964.

Kuhn, Thomas. *Structure of Scientific Revolutions.* Chicago: University of Chicago Press, 1970.

Weber, Max. *The Methodology of the Social Sciences*. Glencoe, Ill.: Free Press, 1949.

The Field Experience

Fichter, Joseph H. *One-Man Research, Reminiscences of a Catholic Sociologist*. New York: Wiley-Interscience, 1973.

Junker, Buford H. *Field Work: An Introduction to the Social Sciences*. Introduction by Everett C. Hughes. Chicago: University of Chicago Press, 1960.

Wax, Rosalie H. *Doing Fieldwork: Warnings and Advice*. Chicago: University of Chicago Press, 1971.

Classic Field Experience Examples

Liebow, Elliot. *Tally's Corner: A Study of Negro Streetcorner Men*. Boston: Little, Brown and Co., 1967.

Morin, Edgar. *The Red and the White: Report from a French Village*, translated by A.M. Sheridan-Smith. New York: Pantheon Books, 1970.

Whyte, William F. *Street Corner Society*. Chicago: University of Chicago Press, 1943.

Wylie, Laurence. *Village in the Vaucluse*. Cambridge, Mass.: Harvard University Press, 1954.

Wylie, Laurence, ed. *Chanzeaux: A Village in Anjou*. Cambridge, Mass.: Harvard University Press, 1966.

General Advice on Collecting Data

Bardach, Eugene. "Gathering Data for Policy Research." *Journal of Urban Analysis* 2 (1974):117–144.

Bernstein, Carl, and Woodward, Robert. *All the President's Men*. New York: Simon & Schuster, 1974.

Charnley, Mitchell V. *Reporting*. New York: Holt, Rinehart and Winston, 1966.

Douglas, Jack D. *Investigative Social Research*. Beverly Hills, Calif.: Sage Publications, 1976.

Johnson, John M. *Doing Field Research*. New York: Free Press, 1975.

Murphy, Jerome T. *Getting the Facts: A Fieldwork Guide for Evaluators and Policy Analysts*. Santa Monica, Calif.: Goodyear, 1980.

Phillips, Bernard S. *Social Research: Strategy and Tactics.* New York: Macmillan, 1971.

Sanders, William B. *The Sociologist as Detective: An Introduction to Research Methods.* New York: Praeger Publications, 1974.

Schatzman, Leonard, and Strauss, Anselm L. *Field Research.* Englewood Cliffs, N.J.: Prentice-Hall, 1974.

Sigal, Leon V. *Reporters and Officials: The Organization and Politics of Newsmaking.* Lexington, Mass.: D. C. Heath & Co., 1973.

Surveys and Sampling

Glock, Charles Y. *Survey Research in the Social Sciences.* New York: Russell Sage Foundation, 1967.

Hyman, Herbert. *Survey Design and Analysis: Principles, Cases, and Procedures.* Glencoe, Ill.: Free Press, 1955.

Leuthold, David A., and Scheele, Raymond J. "Patterns of Bias in Samples Based on Telephone Directories." *Public Opinion Quarterly* 35 (1971):24–57.

Sudman, Seymour. *Applied Sampling.* New York: Academic Press, 1976.

Interviewing

Cannell, Charles F., and Kahn, Robert L. "Interviewing." In *The Handbook of Social Psychology*, edited by Gordon Lindzey and E. Aronson, vol. 2, pp. 526–595. Reading, Mass.: Addison-Wesley, 1968.

Dexter, Lewis A. *Elite and Specialized Interviewing.* Evanston, Ill.: Northwestern University Press, 1970.

Gorden, Raymond L. *Interviewing Strategy: Techniques and Tactics.* Homewood, Ill.: Dorsey Press, 1969.

Hyman, Herbert H. et al. *Interviewing in Social Research.* Chicago: University of Chicago Press, 1975.

Merton, Robert K. et al. *The Focused Interview: A Manual of Problems and Procedures.* Glencoe, Ill.: Free Press, 1956.

Participant-Observation and Passive Observation

Bogdan, Robert, and Taylor, Stephen J. *Introduction to Qualitative Research Methods.* New York: John Wiley & Sons, 1975.

Bruyn, Severyn T. *The Human Perspective in Sociology: The Methodology of Participant Observation.* Englewood Cliffs, N.J.: Prentice-Hall, 1966.

Collier, John, Jr. *Visual Anthropology: Photography as a Research Method.* New York: Holt, Rinehart and Winston, 1967.

Friedrichs, J., and Ludtke, H. *Participant Observation, Theory and Practice.* Lexington, Mass.: D. C. Heath & Co., 1975.

Jacobs, Glenn, ed. *The Participant Observer.* New York: George Braziller, 1970.

McCall, George J., and Simmons, J. L., eds. *Issues in Participant Observation.* Reading, Mass.: Addison-Wesley, 1969.

Schwartz, Morris S., and Green, Charlotte. "Problems in Participant Observation." *American Journal of Sociology* 60, 4 (1955).

Vidich, Arthur J. "Participant Observation and the Collection and Interpretation of Data." *American Journal of Sociology* 60, 4 (1955).

Webb, Eugene J.; Campbell, Donald T.; Schwartz, Richard D.; and Sechrist, Lee. *Unobtrusive Measures: Nonreactive Research in the Social Sciences.* Chicago: Rand McNally & Co., 1966.

Statistics and Quantitative Methods

Alker, Hayward. *Mathematics and Politics.* New York: Macmillan, 1965.

Blalock, Hubert M. *Social Statistics.* 2d rev. ed. New York: McGraw-Hill Book Co., 1979.

Coleman, James S. *Introduction to Mathematical Sociology.* New York: Free Press, 1964.

Doran, J. E., and Hudson, F. R. *Mathematics and Computers in Archaeology.* Cambridge, Mass.: Harvard University Press, 1975.

Edwards, Allen L. *Statistical Methods.* New York: Holt, Rinehart and Winston, 1967.

Hays, W. L. *Statistics for the Social Sciences.* 2d ed. New York: Holt, Rinehart and Winston, 1973.

Kemeny, John G., and Snell, Laurie. *Mathematical Models in the Social Sciences.* Cambridge, Mass.: MIT Press, 1962.

Ostle, Bernard, and Mensing, R. *Statistics in Research.* 3d ed. Ames: Iowa State University Press, 1977.

Comparative Research

Armer, Michael, and Grimshaw, Allen, eds. *Comparative Social Re-*

search: Methodological Problems and Strategies. New York: John Wiley & Sons, 1973.

Holt, Robert T., and Turner, John E., eds. *The Methodology of Comparative Political Research.* Glencoe, Ill.: Free Press, 1970.

Vallier, Ivan, ed. *Comparative Methods in Sociology: Essays on Trends and Applications.* Berkeley: University of California Press, 1973.

Index